When on Earth

Discovering Christian Spirituality in the Daily Happenings of Ordinary Life

A Book of Reflections and Illustrations by

Nina Marie Corona

Copyright 2020 by Nina Marie Corona. All rights reserved.

No part of this publication may be reproduced, distributed, or transmitted in any form without prior written permission of the publisher.

Artwork by Nina Marie Corona (except where otherwise noted)

Cover image used under license from Shutterstock

Book design by www.delaney-designs.com

Editing by www.gloriammarketing.com

Scripture quotations are from the New Revised Standard Version.

ISBN: 978-0-578-63911-6

Printed in the United States of America

www.ninamariecorona.com

For my husband and best friend Mark.

*What a blessing it is to share
the daily happenings of life with you.*

Table of Contents

Preface	11
Introduction	13
When On Earth	17
Lost in Space	21
Reality and Virtuality	25
Show Me Your Truth and I'll Show You Mine	29
To Be or Not to Be	33
The Green Grass of Home	37
Decisions, Decisions, Decisions	41
What Lies Beneath?	45
Kids Are Children Too	47
Like a Cat Out of Hell!	51
Watching Life Go By	53
Mother Knows Best?	57
The Guardian and the Gateway	61
Death Becomes Us	65
Whatever is True	69
Weather or Not	73
Rich Man, Poor Man	75
Hunger Pangs	79
Look Within	83
A Knight in Shining Armor	87
The Remedy for Misery	89
Live Deliberately	93
Living and Learning	97
Enduring the Chore of Change	101
A Girl Can Dream, Can't She?	103
The Fight of Your Life	107

Are You Gonna Carry That Weight? 111
How Does Your Garden Grow? 115
It's Black or White 117
The Inconvenient Truth 121
Who Knows? 125
W.A.I.T. and Listen 129
What Moves You? 131
Fully Alive 135
Success Through Service 137
Life's Waiting Room 141
Trust Me 143
The Reality of Relationships 147
Tapped Out? 151
Training for Simplicity 155
Out of the Darkness 159
A Present or a Privilege? 163
I Resolve…Problem Solved 167
Thanks and Giving 169
Are You For Real??!! 173
Twinkle, Twinkle Little Star 177
We Are But Dust 181
Secular Spirituality 185
The Window to Your Soul 189
All You Need Is Love 191
What's Your Story? 195
See No Evil 199
HIStory 203
The Balancing Act 207

Ignorance is Not Bliss	211
What's Your Instinct?	215
Death and New Life	219
Distinguishing the Giver and the Gifts	221
Now You See It…Now You Don't	225
One Language	227
Life Tightly Woven	231
Foolish Pride	233
Still Learning to Be	237
Day and Night	241
Open to Receive	245
Worthy of Love	249
Lessons From a Tree	253
Loosen Up	255
Let Your Light Shine	259
At the End of Tears	261
The Test of Faith	263
The Tree of Life	267
Leave No Stone Unturned	271
Love Sees	275
A Mother's Day Fairy Tale	277
The Dance	281
Good News	285
Taste and See	287
No Words	291
Saints and Stones	297
Do You Like Me?	301
Walk This Way	305

Preface

These reflections were originally written for a blog that I wrote between 2012 and 2019. During those years I was pursuing my education, first in Studio Arts (B.A.), then Christian Spirituality (M.A.), and finally Ministry (D.Min.). As I pursued God and God's will for my life through academia and my religion, I grappled with the realities of life that were happening around me. From mundane daily events to more difficult circumstances, I prayed, studied, and persevered in faith, hope, and love.

This book does not contain a particular statement or stance; rather it is a glimpse into my heart and soul as I recorded (through words and drawings) my hopes, fears, faith, love, sadness, and more through encounters with the ups and downs of this one life we are all blessed to have. It reveals a small fragment of my faith journey.

If I've learned anything throughout these years of education, I've learned one important thing. We are all the same in that we share common desires, worries, joys, and hopes. We all want to be seen, accepted, and loved. We long for meaning and purpose. Those are the types of reflections you will find in this book, and I hope that you will find they resonate with you because of our "sameness."

After studying about God for over ten years (and counting!), I've learned the rules, the history, the religions, and more. I've prayed with the Bible, read official church documents, and reflected on the words of numerous saints and theologians throughout the ages. Although it took a lot of hard work, a lot of learning, and an awful lot of money, I believe I can speak confidently about God now.

God is love (1 John 4:8).

I pray that in some small way these reflections will draw you nearer to God's love within your own heart, your community, and our planet Earth. I encourage you to spread that love and light widely for all to see and experience.

God bless you.

Introduction

Before I started writing these reflections, spirituality meant something very different to me than it does now. Spirituality meant praying memorized prayers often, going to church daily, studying about my religion, and numerous other religious rituals. My spiritual journey was my quest towards God in Heaven, and it really was somewhat separate from my ordinary life here on Earth. I often felt that I had to pull away from my ordinary life to focus on my spiritual life.

I believe this is a common misconception, and various dictionaries prove the point. Merriam-Webster's online dictionary defines spirituality as, "something that in ecclesiastical law belongs to the church or to a cleric as such." Similarly, the Cambridge Dictionary online defines spirituality as, "the quality that involves deep feelings and beliefs of a religious nature, rather than the physical parts of life." Like my earlier understanding of spirituality, these definitions divide the spiritual from the rest of life (physical or nonreligious).

While studying Christian Spirituality throughout the years, I learned a new definition. Spirituality is simply my "lived experience of faith." It's the way that I experience my faith and how I live it in the day-to-day circumstances of life. When I'm faced with a crisis, frustrated, depressed, or angry, my spirituality is my response to that in light of my faith. Am I able to contextualize the Gospels and bring my faith into the present moment, with all of its ups and downs? Do I invite God into the messes of my life so that I can respond in a more virtuous manner? Do I see the Earth and the people around me through compassionate eyes? Am I working to bring the light of hope into the world and to others? Is love the principle that guides my life? My responses to those questions are some of the ways that I live out my spirituality. This is my lived experience of faith.

Spirituality doesn't always look beautiful or neat and simple, nor does it always feel peaceful as I once assumed. Sometimes it is doubtful, like Thomas before the risen Lord (John 20:24-31). Other times it is restless and lonely (Psalm 102:7). Sometimes it feels thankful and joyful (1Thessalonians 3:9); other times weak and empty (2 Corinthians 12:9). There are even times when it feels like agony, and I've learned that it is then that I might catch a tiny glimpse of faith through the eyes of Jesus' lived experience in the Garden of Gethsemane (Matthew 26:36-46).

Through it all, I persevere here on Earth in my body and all that is attached to that, such as my relationships, my work, my pets, my travels, my feelings, my world, etc. It is here that I experience and live my faith. It is here that I experience God's graces and discover my spirituality in the daily happenings of ordinary life. Through the gifts and fruits of the Holy Spirit,

God wants me to make the Kingdom of God visible here on Earth, as it already is in Heaven (Matthew 6:10).

As you read these reflections, I hope you are able to more fully discover your spirituality in the midst of ordinary days, so that the two may fuse together into one extraordinary life that exudes the unique plan that God has intended just for you.

"Do to others as you would have them do to you."

Luke 6:31

WHEN ON EARTH

I just returned from a cruise (New York - Bermuda - New York). Instead of being left with fond memories of the beautiful teal waters, what seems to be overshadowing is a voice echoing in my head: "When in Rome, do as the Romans do." At each new point of arrival or departure, we were reminded as a group of passengers of how to dress, talk, and behave while on the ship and on the island. These reminders are interesting when you consider the average age of the passengers was around 50 years.

When we boarded the ship, we were reminded to wash our hands, be courteous, and dress properly. In addition to those rules (which one would hope would be common sense), when we arrived in Bermuda, we were told that the islanders would be offended if we did not respond to their cheerful greetings. From what I could tell, most passengers went out of their way to be good little boys and girls, and they behaved themselves. They were kind, clean, and courteous both on the ship and the island.

When we returned to New York after the peaceful seven-day excursion, the rules seemed to automatically switch. Everything changed – the air temperature, the pace, the attitudes, the postures. You could feel the defenses rising as people scrambled to protect themselves and their belongings from internal and external harm. To validate my subconscious senses, the woman behind me in the customs line started snapping her fingers and shouting in a strong New York accent: "COME AWN! LET'S GO! No stopping and looking behind you. We're back in New York now." I turned slowly and glared at her. She laughed and continued arrogantly: "When I was on the island, I was polite and pleasant, but WE'RE BACK NOW... LET'S GO – MOVE IT!"

When we finally made it through customs, we continued to fight through crowds of miserable faces to find our way to the bus. I needed to find a rest room, so I asked a security officer standing nearby. After he gave me directions back into the customs building, I asked him if I needed to bring my passport back in with me. I wish I could show you a video of his response! He looked at me like I was completely out of my mind, made a face to mock me, and gave me a very long drawn out, goofy sounding: "NOOOOOOOOOOOOO" (with the unspoken hint of, YOU IDIOT attached)!!! I responded, staring directly in his eyes, "Stop that. That's very rude!" His attitude changed instantly, and he gave me a warm smile and a hearty laugh. I liked him, even though he probably would have preferred that I didn't.

It was when we finally made it to the bus, loaded our luggage, and found our way to our seats, that the voices started: "You're not in Kansas anymore . . . when in Rome (or New York) . . . etc." And they haven't stopped since.

So this morning I did a little research to see where that saying originated, and to my pleasant surprise, its origin was connected to my favorite saint, Saint Augustine. In his *Letters Volume 1*, he wrote to St. Ambrose, who replied:

"When I visit Rome, I fast on Saturday; when I am here, I do not fast. On the same principle, do you observe the custom prevailing in whatever Church you come to, if you desire neither to give offense by your conduct, nor to find cause of offense in another's."

Wow. "If you desire neither to give offense by your conduct, nor to find cause of offense in another..." Beautiful. Isn't that universal?

Listen, I understand that there are different cultures, paces of life, customs, etc., but we're all on this planet together. We're all the same, and the rules of humanity should be the same everywhere. The rules of common decency and courtesy should be known and practiced everywhere we go from Rome to Bermuda to New York to China to New Zealand and everywhere in between. We need to broaden our perspective to see ourselves from the universe, all on planet Earth. We're all the same! We share the same biological and (for the most part) emotional/spiritual composition. We need to treat each other respectfully with kindness and gentleness wherever we go without instruction.

"Be hospitable to one another without complaining" (1 Peter 4:9). Be polite, kind, and compassionate. Be gentle, cheerful, helpful, and hopeful. Show love, mercy, respect, and concern. Bring these attributes with you wherever you go throughout the entire world. In other words, when on Earth, do as the Earthlings do.

"Those who live at earth's farthest
bounds are awed by your signs;
you make the gateways
of the morning and
the evening
shout for joy."

Psalm 65:8

Lost in Space

I am slowly learning to step back and view things from the big picture. For example, in the midst of some small crisis, I sometimes step back and think, "Right now I'm on a giant ball in the sky, and it's spinning." I can only imagine what we look like from somewhere far off in the universe, bustling around, consumed by our sometimes irrational thoughts, thinking we are the be-all and end-all.

I once said that to my friend. She was going on and on about some trivial thing that was really magnified in her life at the time. I said, "Right now you are on a gigantic ball in the sky that is somehow suspended perfectly in the atmosphere. Anything could happen. At any given moment, we could just start spinning into oblivion!" The distant, troubled look she previously had in her eyes disappeared. She looked at me and forgot what she was talking about.

Look, I know there are things we need to take care of. I understand that we often have real problems. However, the truth of the matter is that most times, there isn't a whole lot we can do about the things that consume us. We worry about things that we have absolutely no control over. We make judgments and statements with such audacity, one would think we are the creators of our environment, and that we know with certainty the M.O. of everything on the face of the earth and perhaps even beyond. We have our two feet planted so firmly and adamantly on the ground that we cannot possibly be moved to see things from another perspective.

The reality is that the true perspective should leave us speechless. It should leave us feeling like children lost in a big amusement park, desperately seeking our parents. Without them, we are wandering aimlessly amidst a vast and complex domain.

What would happen in that scenario if the child lost in the amusement park strutted confidently around perhaps even attempting to run the place? He might explain (to the best of his ability) the mechanics of every ride in the park. "The rides," he might say, "are made of metal and go really fast." Not only that, but he could (in his age-appropriate way) explain the dynamics of every living thing that surrounded him. "The water in the log flume is deep and cold." He is absolutely certain he is right. Perhaps he even is right. Still, there is much he is not capable of knowing at his tender age, and a young child is usually as fairly certain of his limitations as he is of his abilities. That's just one of the attractive qualities of a child.

It would be wonderful if we could live our entire lives like children lost in an amusement park. We would perhaps tread more modestly, while at the same time be filled with joy and excitement. We could eat all the junk food we wanted and go on the dangerous rides, both of which mom and dad would never approve of. However, we'd know that eventually we would be found and pay the price when mom and dad find out what we've done. We'd be wary of strangers who might try to lead us astray. Although it might be fun and exciting, we'd be kind of melancholy at the same time. We'd miss mom and dad, and after a while, we'd just want to go home.

I think that's exactly how we should (and often do) feel but can't decipher. Try it today. In the midst of some small crisis, step back and picture yourself in the infinite universe, lost on the amusement park that is Earth. What's your first impulse in that scenario? It should be to drop to your knees in awe and pray for dear life! It should leave you feeling small, lost, and powerless and open to the guidance and direction of your elders to find your way home. If you keep running, carelessly enjoying the freedom and distracted by the sights and sounds in the "park," you may never find mom and dad.

"Bring the full tithe into the storehouse,
so that there may be food in my house,
and thus put me to the test,
says the Lord of hosts;
see if I will not open the windows
of heaven for you and pour down for you
an overflowing blessing."

Malachi 3:10

Reality and Virtuality

I love technology, maybe because I was young enough to watch its progress and sort of grow with it. My first experience on a computer was when I started working for an airline as a telephone reservations agent in 1981. It was a bulky computer with black background and green type. This is now commonly known as DOS format, but back then it was the only format.

The next seven years were spent in various jobs where I did mainly computer work in the old format. It was not user-friendly, made no logical sense, and it was incredibly boring. At one point I was promoted, and my reward was a memory typewriter! In retrospect, it was a rather silly machine which stored a very small amount of typed data visible on a very tiny screen. It was a fun new toy, but it really didn't have anything exciting to keep me intrigued for long.

When Windows 95 came out, we bought a computer for our home, and I have been hooked ever since. The day that computer arrived I played with it until about 3:00 a.m. I could not believe all of the fun, user-friendly features. Then came the Internet. You can "log in?" What? Access anything, anywhere? That which we now take for granted was almost incomprehensible to me at the time.

So for about the past fifteen years, I can safely bet that not a day has gone by that I haven't been on the computer. Now I have a smartphone. It's really not healthy for someone like me. It's all-consuming. Need the weather? Wait, let me check. Need a recipe? No problem. Counting calories? Check. Need a prayer, a Bible verse, a quote? Got those, too. I even have an app to keep track of the mileage on my sneakers. Go ahead, read that again. You read it correctly.

While I was away last week, I stayed off of the computer entirely, and I left my phone on "airplane mode" to use it only for my downloaded music. No Internet, no calls, no text messages, no distractions. Guess what? I didn't melt. In fact, I realized just how much technology is *taking* from me while I am fooled into thinking it is *giving* to me. I learned that technology has become a false sense of security, identity, and even popularity. It's a false reality, really. I concluded that my self-worth has been attached to the messages I receive or do not receive on my various toys. All of that greatly affects my mood and outlook on any given day.

Maybe it's just me, but I am always checking email, Facebook, phone messages, and text messages. If I get too many messages, I become overwhelmed and anxious. If I don't get any, I feel kind of sad and alone. In essence, I am looking outside of myself, my physical surroundings, and into a realm that doesn't have any real existence (except within my mind and on some computer or phone screen) to connect and feel connected.

But a funny thing happened when I turned it all off. I was actually more connected than ever. I was fully present to the people I was with and much more conscious of my surroundings. I felt more caring. I felt more love. I felt more awake, alive, and present. There were no mood swings, and no sense of isolation even when I was alone. It was just me living fully in the space I was in at any given moment.

Try it sometime. Close the windows on your computer or phone: open up some real windows and look around and within. Breathe. Observe. Listen.

"Be still and know" (Psalm 46:10). You might just find that God had it all covered long before Bill Gates.

"Little children,
let no one deceive you.
Everyone who does what is
right is righteous,
just as he is righteous."

1 John 3:7

Show Me Your Truth and I'll Show You Mine

It's so difficult to have a relationship, isn't it? Any relationship, not just romantic ones. They are so complex. It sometimes feels like a game of chess in which each person is quietly contemplating his or her next move and anticipating what the other's responding move will be. It takes effort, concentration, intuition, and intelligence. It's all quite the challenge.

The game of chess is fun and exciting because in the end there will be a winner who outsmarts the loser. In the game of life and friendship, the prospect of being the loser is not a matter to be toyed with. It's not a game, and it shouldn't be played as such.

I've had friends throughout the years who played our relationship like a game of chess. One in particular really stands out to this day, although it was over thirty years ago. The relationship was such a chore – like the game – yet I kept playing for some odd reason. Maybe I didn't know better, and I thought that was just the way it was supposed to be. Perhaps I was afraid to be alone and without friends. We talked frequently on the phone and went out to bars, the mall, the movies, etc. We even worked together. However, the entire relationship was a game of chess. It took so much effort, and I was constantly trying to contemplate the next move.

One day I caught this "friend" in a lie. It was the silliest thing to lie about, and the situation behind the lie had no direct impact on our relationship. However, the fact that this person felt it necessary to lie to me really upset me. Don't get me wrong; I was far from perfect. I've been a horrible friend to others in the past. I played the game as well. Hey, it was all about protecting my queen, right? I was born and raised in Newark, NJ. I know how to protect myself.

In recent years, I've received an amazing gift: the gift of truth. There is nothing so pure and freeing as the truth, and there is no better fertilizer for a friendship. If I want to play a game, I'll play chess. If I want to be in a relationship – to share, grow, learn, love, play, smile, cry – I'll find a friend. I'll find someone who is not afraid to show me his or her truth. I'll find people who take off their masks and show me their scars, and I'll do the same.

When it's all out there – the whole truth (and nothing but the truth please!) – there are no winners or losers. It's not about playing; it's about sharing, flawed individuals sharing their truths. There are no winners or losers because NOTHING can beat that.

*"So then, putting away falsehood,
let all of us speak the truth
to our neighbors,
for we are members
of one another."*

Ephesians 4:25

"For it is written,
"You shall be holy, for I am holy."

1 Peter 1:16

To Be or Not to Be

Several years ago, I went back to school to study theology and philosophy. Midway through my education, I decided to change my major to studio arts. A year later, I was questioning that decision. I'd been on break for two weeks, and I had only picked up a paintbrush one day. Yet for some unknown reason, I'd also started writing a blog. Here I was, fifty years-old, still trying to figure out what I wanted to be. Did you get that contradiction? *Here I **am** trying to figure out what I want to **be**.*

This kind of contradiction had been going on for years. I graduated high school in 1980 and was accepted into Montclair State College. My major was undecided, but I was leaning strongly towards art. I commuted to college and worked part time at a supermarket, making more than eight dollars per hour. It was good pay back then, and I didn't feel like sitting in school for four years when I could be working full time and earning money. So I left college and decided to go to business school for a year to study "airline and travel." Yes, there was actually an entire course for that. I was hired as a telephone sales agent for World Airways immediately after graduation, and I absolutely hated it. I sat at a computer in a dismal office at the not-so-scenic Newark International Airport for about ten hours a day. It was repetitive work and BORING! It was certainly not the glamorous world I envisioned.

My marriage and move to Florida (see the Green Grass of Home reflection) rescued me from that monotony. I wouldn't even consider seeking work in the airline industry again in Florida. So I decided to put my administrative skills to the test. I quickly got a job at a large newspaper in the classified advertising department. My job title had something to do with "pagination," which was a fancy title for inputting a bunch of stuff in the computer. It was just as boring as my work at the airport, and my supervisor was extremely difficult to work with. That discontent led me to transfer to the personnel department as some sort of an administrative assistant, which was a fancy title for "sitting in an office doing nothing." I was bored again. So I transferred to the affiliated magazine as an administrative assistant to the editor and publisher. That was fun for a few months until the guy I worked for transferred to the Washington Post. Back to boredom I went.

In 1988, I gave birth to my first daughter. Motherhood kept me challenged and gratified. When my youngest daughter started kindergarten, however, my quest began again. What was I going to be? There was absolutely nothing in the classifieds that appealed to me, so I took a chance and started my own food manufacturing business. That, my friends, is a book unto itself, so I will not even go there. All I will tell you is that the business kept me preoccupied (I *didn't* say satisfied) for about twelve years before the nagging feeling that there was still something more I was missing returned.

All of those experiences led to the contradiction, "Here I am trying to figure out what I want to be." My spiritual director has reminded me more than once that I am a human *being*, not a human *doing*. I am not what I do. I simply "am." I am worthy of life and love simply because I am. I am not who I am because of what I do or do not do. My husband too keeps reminding me to enjoy the journey and stop worrying about the destination. The journey has been awesome, but I've spent so much time thinking about the destination (what I'm going to be) that I am not fully enjoying the adventure, and I really don't appreciate who I am at any given point throughout the journey.

I have to admit that the most gratified I have ever been is when I become so absorbed in something outside of myself that I forget all about myself. It all goes back to the cup reflection (see I Need a Drink reflection). I can't fill myself. There is nothing I can do that will fill that inner longing. I can only be. While I am being, the best way to experience gratification is through dying to myself and my desires. It's the greatest paradox, but in it lies everything we seek. In Luke 9:23-24, Jesus says: "If any want to become my followers, let them deny themselves and take up their cross daily and follow me. For those who want to save their life will lose it, and those who lose their life for my sake will save it."

Shakespeare was right. "To be or not to be" really is the question, not "to do or not to do." So I'm challenging myself to be open to what life has to offer me daily. To be joyful and grateful and hopeful. To be and feel worthy and loveable and loving. To be alive and present. To be caring and compassionate. To be holy and good.

To be or not to be? I think I'll choose "to be" since I already "am."

"Take delight in the Lord,
and he will give you
the desires of your heart."

Psalm 37:4

The Green Grass of Home

Twenty-nine years ago, at the age of twenty-one, I got married and moved from New Jersey to Florida the very next day. It was an exciting time of planning and dreaming. For months before the wedding and move, visions of palm trees and sunny skies danced in my head as I daydreamed while staring out the window of Newark International Airport, where I worked. My husband and I were going to get away from all of "this." New, and beautiful places, new faces, and a happily ever after in paradise. A friend of mine came to say goodbye to me the day I was leaving. She started crying, and at the time, I couldn't imagine why.

I soon understood. I spent the next six-plus years crying and complaining about the heat, the tourists, and the old people, while greatly missing family, friends, familiar places, and the four seasons.

After the birth of our first daughter, my husband and I finally broke out of the routine of life to move back up north. Once again, the daydreaming started as I watched that Newhart show based in Vermont again. Hurray! We were headed back to the snow, the seasons, the mountains, the trees—even real dirt and rocks were appealing! It was all going to be so wonderful, just like the show. Don't laugh, but my husband even took a job transfer to Vermont. It was a town called St. Johnsbury, situated at the northern tip of Vermont near the Canadian border. We packed up to leave, and as before, family and friends came teary-eyed to say goodbye. Adios! It's been real, but we're outta here!

So the trek began from the south of the country to the very north. My husband drove a rented trailer with all of our belongings, and I drove our vehicle with our most precious belonging, our daughter. We smiled and dreamed and drove... and drove, and drove, and drove. After a while, it started to seem quite far—too far. My smile disappeared somewhere around Connecticut, but we kept driving. At one point in Vermont, the radio stations pretty much disappeared, and there was one religious station. Then, in the middle of the night, an old black station wagon with white skulls painted on it drove past me. Where in the world was I??!

When we finally arrived in St. Johnsbury, it was about 2:00 a.m. The motel we had reserved left the key out for us, and we proceeded to our very simple room. The next morning, we drove around to check out the town. It was early October. It was already cold, and there was no sign that there had ever been life on the trees. There was one grocery store, and half of the people in it (that would be about six) spoke French. Forget this. I wasn't going to spend another six years in misery. I told my husband that he could stay if he wanted, but that I was heading back to New Jersey with our daughter. The poor guy didn't have a choice. He told the hiring manager that we weren't staying, and we left (now homeless and jobless) for New Jersey. Thank God my husband was able to get a position with his company in New Jersey. We lived there for a year while we searched for a home in Pennsylvania. We've been in PA ever since.

All that experience didn't stop us from daydreaming again when we were in Bermuda last week. Crystal-clear waters, sunny skies, pink houses, fresh fish daily, and mopeds! Wouldn't life be grand? One day while we were enjoying ice cream at a local parlor, a native Bermudian named Eleanor approached us. "Do you love our island? It's beautiful, isn't it? I was born here. The people are wonderful." We agreed, and the conversation continued to the shopping, which led to the high cost of living, which led to a discussion of Costa Rica, where Eleanor and her husband hoped to live someday.

She said: "Pineapples there are only 50 cents apiece. They are $7.00 here. Plus, we can purchase land in Costa Rica for only $35,000.00. We are going to retire there soon." Before long she was explaining that all of the shops in Bermuda close at 5:00 pm. "There's nothing to do here in the evening." She continued: "If you want to leave, you have to take a plane somewhere. It's quite monotonous sometimes." By the end of the conversation, my husband and I couldn't wait to get off of that island!

We're funny creatures, we humans. We're always searching. We think: "There's got to be something better than this. Life will be great when . . ." It's the old, "the grass is greener on the other side" syndrome. The truth is that we're seeking happiness externally that can only be found internally. The ultimate happiness that we seek, whether it be a person, place, or thing, is not going to be found anywhere on this Earth. No amount of sunshine is going to fill that spot of darkness that always seems to loom.

You see, there is no person who can truly complete us. There is no place that will make us feel as if we are truly where we belong. There is no thing that is going to fill that emptiness, that longing. There is a hole in our souls that is, as they say, God-sized.

St. Augustine said it best: "Our hearts are restless, O Lord, until they rest in you." Until we reach our final destination, my experience has taught me that every place is different. No place is perfect. And there's no place like home.

"After you have made a decision
that is pleasing to God,
the Devil may try to make you
have second thoughts.
Intensify your prayer time,
meditation, and good deeds.
For if Satan's temptations merely
cause you to increase your efforts
to grow in holiness,
he'll have an incentive
to leave you alone."

Saint Ignatius of Loyola

Decisions, Decisions, Decisions

I've never been good at making decisions. When I was growing up, my mom used to say: "What are you going to do when you have to make *real* decisions?!" I'm ridiculous really. Food shopping is a nightmare for me. As soon as I walk into a large supermarket, I am swept into an altered state bordering on delirium! My eyes start darting back and forth, and I can't seem to move three feet without being sidetracked by some enormous display or sample presentation. It's all too much. I just need a few items, and I have to make my way through mayhem starting in the parking lot.

Even before entering the building, the decisions begin. "Should I carry a basket, take a small cart, or do I need a large cart? Ugh! I forgot the reusable bags (every single time)!" I'm not frazzled yet, so I make that decision confidently and start walking past huge displays of water and soda of every shape, size, flavor, and color. They are all in plastic though, so I have to take some time to see if the plastic is BPA-free or not. "To heck with it. I'll just get that on the way out." I move another five feet or so, and I come across beautiful strawberries. I don't need them, but they look so good. Wait, they're not organic. Now I start looking for the organic ones. As I wander around wondering about the pesticides used on all the beautiful fruits and vegetables, I remember that I am not here for strawberries. I refocus and move on. "Where's the darn lettuce? Oh, there it is." Now the real confusion begins. There's green leaf, red leaf, romaine, Bibb, spring mix, and iceberg (and that's just the tip of the iceberg!). I have to decide if I want the prepackaged or loose – organic or poisoned – bulk package or single – on and on it goes.

Somehow I make that decision, but I haven't left the produce aisle unscathed. Although I think I can still pull off looking sane, the short-circuiting in the brain has begun (I call it sensory overload). I press onward through the grocery aisles (all twenty-five of them) keeping my head tilting downward so I don't get tempted to stop to consider the endless sale signs popping out from every direction. I've got this now; I'm going to get the orange juice and get out. God help me: the dairy case is at least fifty feet long, and the orange juices comprise about half of that. I stare blankly at the selections. I'm not sure. I really just want orange juice! There's pulp, no pulp, extra pulp, extra vitamins, calcium, various flavors, brands, prices, sizes, etc. This isn't funny anymore! Who is toying with me?! As I become more and more bewildered, a woman comes up next to me, grabs a carton, and starts walking away. I mumbled something like: "Is this really necessary? I just want orange juice!" To which she replies: "You just can't make a decision!" Ouch! Now not only am I dazed, frazzled, and confused; I've also lost any self-esteem I had when I walked into the darn building.

I'm not sure mom was right. *Real* decisions come easier to me. It's life or death, a no-brainer. But somewhere along the way, we were given way too many choices. Things were simpler when we knew where we had to live, work, go to school, etc. We didn't have a choice, and we made the best of it. Now we are constantly wanting something other than what we have because oftentimes there are many choices, too many. We usually end up thinking we made the wrong one or wondering what might be if we choose differently yet again. It's all too complex. For my sanity, simplicity trumps complexity every time.

*"Do not store up for yourselves
treasures on earth,
where moth and rust consume
and where thieves
break in and steal."*

Matthew 6:19

What Lies Beneath?

Have you ever thought about the depth of the ocean? When I was on a cruise ship years ago, the ocean depth was nearly 17,000 feet at one point. My daughter told me that the deepest part of the ocean is over 35,000 feet. The vastness is exciting and a bit frightening at the same time. It's a place where light doesn't shine, and it seems to me that only something creepy could survive in that. The photos I've seen on the Internet of some of those creatures confirm that idea. They are strange and look almost mutated. Things hidden in darkness may be ugly, or their beauty simply cannot be seen. Once the light shines on them, they either lose their power to scare us, or their beauty shines forth.

What if the entire ocean was somehow drained, and everything within it was exposed? There's an old children's book that I used to love called *The Five Chinese Brothers*. At one point in the story, one of the brothers swallowed the ocean. I used to love that page of the book where the ocean floor was revealed. It read: "All the treasures of the sea lay uncovered." Think about that. Once the mysterious, dark, and shadowing waters were purged, whatever remained exposed lost its obscurity and even became valuable.

I don't know about you, but I prefer not to swim in the ocean where I cannot see what's swimming with me. My imagination runs wild, and I envision all kinds of frightening creatures waiting to take a bite out of me. I've often said: "I'll go into the deep ocean water only when I can wear steel tubes on my legs!" I'm afraid of those monsters hiding beneath – unexposed to the light – that might prey on and devour me.

Sure, there's something quite adventurous about it all. The mystery of the unknown and unpredictable can be quite intriguing. The mystery attracts us, but with the absence of the light exposing the reality within, we really are intrigued with a fantasy, one that can be quite dangerous.

All of this gets me thinking about what *we* keep hidden within, unexposed to the light. It's kind of like swimming in the ocean, surrounded by others whom we really cannot see. Their physical bodies are present, but the true depths of their souls remain hidden deep, because they are afraid what is revealed might seem ugly or mutated. Likewise, we may be intrigued by the mystery surrounding people, but we must remember that until the depths are revealed, it's all just a fantasy.

Ultimately, everything will be exposed to the Light. St. Paul wrote: "He will bring into the light of day all that at present is hidden in darkness, and He will expose the secret motives of men's hearts" (1 Corinthians 4:5). Like the ocean floor in the book *The Five Chinese Brothers*, our souls will ultimately reveal our hidden shipwrecks and treasures. It would be wonderful and wise if we start exposing what we're hiding while we're still here on the earth. The hidden mutations that we are afraid to reveal might look beautiful once they've been exposed to the light. The shipwrecks can be explored, the debris can be cleared, and the treasures that remain can be shared with all.

> *"Truly I tell you, unless you change and become like children, you will never enter the kingdom of heaven."*
>
> **Matthew 18:3**

Kids Are Children Too

When my daughters were very young, I was constantly trying to persuade them to jump rope. They hated it, but I kept buying ropes throughout the years, hoping that eventually they would see the joy in it. I used to love to jump rope when I was a kid. It was one of my favorite activities, along with bike riding, playing tag, and hopscotch. That was all true, but I also told my girls that I was an excellent student: always did my homework, got good grades, was never late, etc. Then one day my youngest found my report card from high school. She brought it to me and, with a surprised look on her face, said: "Mom! You told me you were a great student! Look at your grades! And you were always absent or late!" Oops...

Throughout the years, I continued to encourage them to join all kinds of activities. Unlike jumping rope though, these were activities that I had never done as a child, but it was "the thing to do" when my children were being raised. God forbid your child wasn't involved in a sport, theater program, or playing an instrument (better if all three). My girls felt the pressure from their peers, teachers, and other adults, and I felt the pressure from society. To be a good parent meant to run your kids from activity to activity, always expecting them to be the best (and I don't mean their personal best). My eldest daughter would have preferred to stay home and read books, but I was constantly trying to push her out of her comfort zone. Of course, it was all in her best interest, because this was what society expected. What rubbish.

One day I was talking to my friend on the phone, and she said: "Suzie won't join anything except cheering, and I don't think cheering is a very good activity for her to have on her college application." I think the girls were in middle school at the time – okay, to make it sound reasonable, let's say they were in high school. These types of conversations continued for years, and my eldest daughter would rarely join anything. The poor thing tried basketball one year, and she was traumatized by the experience. She was not an athlete by any means (oh the horror!), but she tried her best. The other kids and their parents weren't interested in her personal best – they wanted to win – and they let her know about it. Prior to that she tried softball, and the parents were so nasty that I stopped going to watch the games. I think about that now, and I wonder what I was thinking. I didn't go because I couldn't handle it, but I expected my daughter to not only tolerate it, but to try to perform as these insane people expected.

One day I finally said to my friend: "Why the heck are we doing this to our kids? What did we do when we were in school?" We both laughed at the fact that we would *never* have joined any of the activities that our kids were involved in, and in fact, we were never involved in an activity at all. We turned out okay, right? My friend explained to me that it's a whole new world, and the kids needed to do these things in order to succeed. She added: "There's a lot of competition out there, and they have to play the game." Of course, I wanted my girls to succeed, so I continued to try to encourage them to get involved.

What a mixed-up society we are. Why on God's good earth must children be more than anything except children? It is the one time in life when we are free to just be carefree, simple, relaxed with no worries, major responsibilities, or pressures. When I think back to my childhood, I remember backyard carnivals, snowball fights, movie nights, games, bubble gum, and chocolate milk. I think of running, playing, and laughing. I recall Jerry Lewis, Abbot and Costello, and *I Love Lucy*. I remember trips to the mountains, the shore, the park, and the zoo. Thank God I was allowed to be a child. Then I was permitted to be a typical teenager. Finally, I had to grow up and become an adult. And to think – I did all of that without even one formal activity on my college application.

"This is the day
that the Lord has made;
let us rejoice and be glad in it."

Psalm 118:24

Like a Cat Out of Hell!

We should all see the world through the eyes of my daughter's cat. Romeo rises every morning at 5:00 am with a skip in his step. He's had a good night's rest, and he's ready for a full breakfast. The rest of the day, he appears to be engaged in either complete relaxation (the likes of which I think I'll never know), or utter fascination. He lives totally in the present moment and enjoys everything fully.

Occasionally, I carry Romeo outside to have a look around and a breath of fresh air. At first, he was afraid, and he would cling to me for dear life as he hesitatingly peeked over my shoulders to have a look around. Eventually, the peeks became wide-eyed gawks as if he couldn't believe what he was seeing. The bug-eyes eventually diminished, but then his head started twisting around 360 degrees to try to take it all in. Finally, he was ready to explore on his own, and he tried to wiggle his way out of my arms. So I put him on the ground to feel the dirt and rocks (while still holding onto him). He was happy at first just sitting still and looking.

Then one night, Romeo took off like a cat out of hell and went running down the street. No looking back, no gawking – just running as if he knew exactly where he was going. Then he stopped and hid under some bushes where my daughter finally caught him and brought him back to our prison/home. I have no doubt that he will be looking to escape daily from now on. There's a whole world out there for him to explore, and he's onto it now!

It's a new and beautiful day. There are countless things to see, to explore, and to enjoy. So let's rise with a skip in our steps, have a full breakfast, and run like cats out of hell from our prisons/homes to see, explore, and play! Let's marvel at God's creation, as though seeing the world for the first time. Don't plan and think too much. Be spontaneous and just run like you know exactly where you're going. It'll be fun!

> *"The thief comes only to steal and kill and destroy. I came that they may have life, and have it abundantly."*
>
> **John 10:10**

Watching Life Go By

After years of obnoxiously clicking the remote control; after decades of complaining, "There's nothing on;" after a lifetime of absorbing mindless, needless, violent, sexual, subliminal, degrading, depressing, and just plain ludicrous images and information, we finally canceled the cable service in our household.

One night soon after we canceled cable, while at the gym, a woman had the television on and was watching a romantic movie. I watched for a while and realized I've really missed those Tampax commercials. Ugh.

The truth is that we haven't missed television at all. We do have one television in our home, and it is connected via wireless to Netflix. We now have the freedom to choose the movie, documentary, or television shows that we want, when we want, without being fed a steady diet of trash and being subjected to countless hours of annoying and even disgusting commercials. We don't have to accidentally absorb violent or sexual images while trying to find some decent entertainment. We don't get sucked into watching the latest popular reality shows. We are not brainwashed by the news media. We are not hypnotized by the sights, sounds, sales, and storms. The best part is we are no longer paying over $75 a month for all that aggravation.

This was just another one of those things that I'd wanted to do for years, but I was afraid to go against the grain. Television is such a part of our culture that even the discussion of removing it confuses people. "What will you do at night? How will you stay informed? You'll miss The Jersey Shore!"

I actually was convinced that I'd be missing something, that my life would be "less than." People would say, "I always have the television on. The noise keeps me company." Maybe it's me, but I do not find background noise comforting. I need the interaction of a real, live person to keep me company. Though I definitely can understand how the elderly, or someone who is convalescing, bedridden, or otherwise housebound might find the television quite distracting and/or comforting, many of us are in no such predicament. We are simply doing what we've always done and what society tells us is normal.

Television is far from normal. In fact, it has gotten so out of control that it is downright abnormal. It is no longer first and foremost a source of entertainment, but rather a vehicle to confuse and manipulate us. We have allowed the media to increasingly push the envelope to the point where we are desensitized to things that should outrage us. There are no moral values or boundaries. The stings become stronger and more blatant, but we just allow them to keep stinging. Eventually, we no longer feel the pain. We are where they want us to be. Somehow, we've convinced ourselves that we are in charge and that we want this. We pay money for it, and we purchase larger and larger appliances to house it all. Aren't we the lucky ones to have this luxury?

The power is back in my hands where it belongs, and I am certainly no worse for the wear. If I want to read the news, I buy a newspaper or turn on the Internet. If I want entertainment, I choose something that meets my standards on Netflix. If I need "background noise," I turn on the radio. If I want company, I call someone. I have more time, more money, and more control. It's not like I have forever on this planet. I can certainly find better uses for my time and money. Instead of watching live television, I prefer to just live life.

I really miss the Tampax, Viagra, and Depends commercials though.

"Train children in the right way,
and when old, they will not stray."

Proverbs 22:6

Mother Knows Best?

I don't know why it is said that "Mother knows best." I never felt like I knew much of anything. I can so vividly remember the day I was sent home from the hospital with my first newborn daughter in my arms. It had all been such a beautiful and safe experience up to that point. Of course, there were moments of pain and fear, but I felt that I was in good hands with professionals who understood the birthing process and would care for me and the baby. They showed me how to hold the baby and breastfeed and how to wrap the baby in a receiving blanket. They brought the baby in only for feedings and took her to the nursery when she cried. It was all so beautiful.

Then suddenly two days after this major life experience (while I was still in serious discomfort from an episiotomy), they put me in a wheelchair with the baby and sent us on our merry way. It felt surreal. My husband and I were in our mid-twenties. We had no idea what the heck to do from that moment on. Decades later, we still don't have a clue.

In fact, mothering is one of the few situations in which I feel completely powerless. I was never in control. From the very moment of conception, it was all out of my hands. I had two miscarriages, so fear was usually predominant, especially in the first trimester. For nine months, I waited anxiously as this being grew within me.

All I could control was what I consumed, though oftentimes I even seemed to have no control over that. Weird cravings hit at odd times of the day and night. It might sound cute, but it wasn't. When I had a craving, it was as if an alien possessed me. I had no control. This thing wanted hot dogs and anything else that contained nitrates. I was big into health food at the time, but I had no control. I ate the hot dogs and pepperoni.

I waited patiently as my body warped inside and out. It was a time of hope and trust, fear and faith, mystery and intrigue, wonder and awe. Words could never describe the beauty of the birthing process. The body is so amazing, and all the intellect in the world is pretty much worthless when it comes to the birthing process. There's not much you can do except sit back and wait for the body to do what it is going to do while praying that what comes out is human. A miracle happens every single time a baby is born.

Somewhere along the way I guess I forgot that feeling of powerlessness, and I started forcing my control. It's all with the best of intentions, of course. We're in no-win situations, we mothers. You have to look at it from our perspective. We're to discipline, yet forgive; protect, yet release; guide, yet detach. We're expected to know everything, then we're told we know nothing. We're expected to be available, but we're told to get our own lives.

It's all very confusing, and I personally can never believe how seriously my kids take me! My youngest daughter and I were talking just last week, and I was apologizing for something I said recently. Then I thought about it and said: "I can't believe you take me that seriously!" My daughter laughed and replied: "You're my mom!" I was not much older than she is now when I was pregnant. Funny, isn't it? I replied: "I'm just like you, but I had a child. I wasn't given all the answers – just the child. I do the best I can."

I think the saying should be changed from: "Mother knows best" to something like, "Mother does her best with the best of intentions and all of her love." That's the truth, and hopefully that's enough.

"But Jesus said,
"Let the little children come to me,
and do not stop them;
for it is to such as these
that the kingdom of heaven belongs."

Matthew 19:14

The Guardian and the Gateway

I remember when I went to see *To Rome With Love*. One of the characters sort of traveled back in time and met himself as a young boy. It was an interesting and rather unnerving thing to observe this middle-aged businessman hanging out with himself as a young college guy. It really got me thinking, what would "little Nina" think of "big Nina" if she were to meet her now? Would I be a disappointment to the little girl who had big dreams for life? Would she thank me for taking care of her and for keeping her dreams alive? Would she be sad and feel that I had "sold out" like the young man in the movie?

Inside of all of us dwells a little child who once jumped, played, laughed, and danced. This child had big hopes and dreams, and she knew that anything was possible. She was excited about the opportunities that lay ahead. She had this one, seemingly endless life to live with so many exciting possibilities.

I wanted to be a figure skater, a pianist, a dancer, or an artist. I wanted to somehow leave a mark on the world, my own personal handprint. I had many dreams, and my dreams knew no limits. Anything was possible.

If I could take that same little girl physically by the hand and take a walk with her today, how would the conversation go? What would she think as she looked up at me? Would I be someone she admired; someone she would aspire to be like? If she asked me if I did all of those things that she really wanted to do, could I respond "yes?" Could I tell her that the dream was true, and that I worked hard to make of this life what she imagined it could be?

Instead, would I be jaded, angry, and cynical? Would I tell her that is was all a fantasy and that "real life" is too difficult for me to manage and give her what she wanted? Would I tell her to "go away and leave me to deal with the harsh realities of a cruel world?"

I think that I would love to spend the day with little Nina, and that she would love to spend the day with me. I could tell her funny stories of ice-skating lessons and Irish dance classes that I took as an adult. I would tell her that I am still working hard to make those same pictures that she drew in her bedroom, and I would show her all of the new and exciting ways I have learned to make them. I could tell her a wild and crazy story about what I did with her Nana's rice pudding recipe. I would tell her that anything really is possible, and I have kept her dreams alive and well. I have taken care of her body, mind, and spirit. I think she would be proud, and she would love me.

Take out a photo of yourself as a child. Spend some time alone remembering who you were, what your hopes and dreams were. Then take a good, hard, sincere look in the mirror. This isn't a time for excuses, blame, or guilt. This is simply a time of purity and truth. You might be angry at what the child had to endure, but he has in fact endured. There may have been things you could not protect him or her from, but you are here now to be the protector. There may have been devastating losses and difficult circumstances, but you are here now to be the nurturer.

This is also a time of opportunity to give the child hope. It's an opportunity to start over and become the person your little child can admire and look up to. It's an opportunity to offer a special child an attitude of acceptance, peace, and hope. You are the child's guardian and the gateway.

"Commit your work to the Lord,
and your plans will be established."

Proverbs 16:3

Death Becomes Us

My academic advisor once asked me what I envisioned myself doing in five years. It was an interesting and annoying question.

I don't think I've ever had a clear vision at any point in my life of where I would like to be in five years. In many ways, I feel like I fly through life by the seat of my pants. Though I always seem to have some major project going on, I don't really think of a career as being a goal. When I think of my life beyond the day-to-day stuff, I think of the big picture—the really big picture. What will my life have meant when it's over?

So then the question becomes, what is my goal for my life, and how can I get closer to that during the next five years? Lately I feel like I'm running out of time. Age has a way of doing that to a person. We do die, you know.

I can remember as a child discovering that I was going to die. I was truly perplexed and disturbed! It was unfathomable to me, and I was absolutely certain that it couldn't be true. I remember thinking immediately about what I could do to leave a mark so that people in the future will know that I was here. It wasn't about vanity; it was just that I felt like I had some value, something beyond matter, something *that* mattered. I didn't want to waste away like a flower or a tree branch having had no real significance, and I had a strong sense that my life had a deep meaning and real purpose.

The definition of death is: "The end of life; the total and permanent cessation of all the vital functions of an organism." I am an organism that will eventually stop working and being. I will wither and die, and my body will decompose. Parts of its remains will be utilized in other systems. It's scientifically fascinating really, but we somehow innately know as human beings that there is more to us than that. I knew it as a young child. Nobody told me, but I had a very strong natural awareness of that. The problem is that we feel a sense of entitlement to life. We forget (or don't even consider) that we didn't have to be born. Each and every day is a gift that was given to us. If we are given any other material gift that eventually stops working, we don't curse the day we were given it! We are usually grateful to the giver of the gift and for the time we were able to use it.

It is interesting how shocked we are when people die. It's like we've been duped! People have been dying since the beginning of time. It's the only real guarantee that we have. Yet it disturbs and even angers us, as if we deserve better. Though it's inevitable, we often prefer not to think about it or discuss it. It's too morbid.

I myself find it fascinating, and I believe we live our best lives in the constant light/awareness of death. As John Oxenham said, "For death begins with life's first breath - And life begins at touch of death." Contrary to that idea, we tend to live our lives as if they are infinite, and when we discover death is impending, we are shocked, angry, and begin to either think of all the things we could have done or begin doing things we want to do before we die.

So, where do I envision myself in five years? Well, a villa in Tuscany sounds nice, but would that really matter? I envision myself still seeking, asking, knocking, hoping, reaching out, and struggling to rise above and beyond the organism that is me. I'll let you know if I ever reach my goal. How about you?

"And everyone who lives and believes in me will never die. Do you believe this?"

John 11:26

"When the Spirit of truth comes,
he will guide you into all the truth;
for he will not speak on his own,
but will speak whatever he hears,
and he will declare to you
the things that are to come."

John 16:13

WHATEVER IS TRUE

St. Paul wrote: ". . . whatever is true, whatever is honorable, whatever is just, whatever is pure, whatever is pleasing, whatever is commendable, if there is any excellence and if there is anything worthy of praise, think about these things." (Philippians 4:8). Wow! Who talks like that? Wouldn't you love to meet this guy? Is there anyone on the face of the earth nowadays who can even understand what those adjectives mean, much less act upon those words? If you can, please, speak up now; your voice is desperately needed.

Who is to determine what exactly is true, honorable, just, pure, lovely, gracious, and excellent? Could it be that my idea of the truth is different than your idea? Is there such a thing as "my truth" and "your truth," or is there simply truth? I believe that there is but one common truth (love), and I believe we have lost sight of it in a big way in society. We've lost it in such a big way, in fact, that we couldn't see the truth if it smacked us upside the head. I don't believe that "my truth" can be different than "your truth" because there is in fact one common truth, and if we are all seeking that same one truth, then there can be no discrepancy. If I focus on "whatever is true, honorable, just, pure, lovely, gracious, excellent, and worthy of praise," and you are focused on the same, how can we not peaceably arrive at the truth? It should be crystal clear, simple, pure, lovely, etc.

Where do we turn to find out exactly what the truth is? In courts, we still have to place our hand on a Bible to "swear the whole truth and nothing but the truth." However, we all know that the truth is not always told in court. In fact, in a court case where there is a plaintiff and a defendant, all are swearing to tell the truth, yet obviously someone is going to be lying. If they were all telling the actual truth, there would be no case to begin with (generally speaking). Since someone is lying, the plaintiff tells "his truth," and the defendant tells "her truth," and hopefully the judge will find "the truth."

I think the solution lies in the question. If it is not lovely, gracious, pure, just, and honorable, then it is not true. If the fruit of the situation bears an adjective that is opposite of those, it is untrue, and it needs to be avoided. Whatever is disagreeable, cowardly, partial, hateful, mixed, these things are not heading in any way, shape, or form towards truth, and these are the things we need to shy away from if we are seeking the truth.

St. Paul gave us another wonderful quote about the fruit of the Spirit (and of course the Spirit is true). He said: "But the fruit of the Spirit is love, joy, peace, forbearance, kindness, gentleness, and self-control" (Galatians 5:22-23). If you can place your head on a pillow at night when faced with the truth, and you are filled with the fruits of the Spirit, that is your indicator of the truth, and that will be enough to face a world of darkness and lies. That is God's grace, and that is the only real judge and jury of the truth. How well do you sleep at night?

*"And you will know the truth,
and the truth will make you free."*

John 8:32

"Whoever observes the wind
will not sow;
and whoever regards the clouds
will not reap."

Ecclesiastes 11:4

Weather or Not

I wonder why we are so obsessed with the weather. I know it's not just me because there are television and radio stations, apps, and websites dedicated to just the weather. We have temperature gauges in our homes, cars, and offices.

Sure, there are times when it comes in handy. Maybe we are planning a long ride, and we'd prefer not to travel if there is an impending monsoon. For the most part though, our daily fixation with the weather is really unnecessary, unreasonable, and unproductive. Let's not forget to mention that it's usually incorrect as well!

I am always looking at the 10-day forecast. Call me anytime, and I can tell you what the temperature and sky conditions will be on any given day. More than fifty percent of the time it's wrong, but I've stored it in my brain for some beneficial purpose that has not yet revealed itself. It's quite pointless. If I would look up a new word, give someone a call, do a few squats, or say a prayer as often as I check the weather, I'd be a heck of a lot more productive.

I used to read The Berenstain Bears to my girls. One of the books was called *The Berenstain Bears and Too Much TV*. Mama decided that the entire family was watching too much television, and they were all getting fat, lazy, and uncreative. Papa chimed in: "How will we know what the weather will be?" To which Mama smartly replied: "Try this, it's called putting your hand out the window to see if it's raining!" What a novel idea.

We think we're so smart and so progressive, but we're going backwards in all of the ways that really matter. Our gadgets keep us enslaved in such a subliminal way that we don't even realize what's happening.

One of the most destructive things about it all is that we are kept from living fully in the present. To look outside, open the window or door, and see and feel the weather is much more enlightening and stimulating than checking it on a gadget. It creates a level of awareness that involves our entire being and all of our senses, not just our mind. Instead, we're letting our gadgets dictate our lives, our moods, our plans, and our time. We are feeding off of textual and pictorial stimuli on a screen rather than being present in and aware of our surroundings.

I'm trying to live more fully in the present and to be aware of what is happening around me. But in case you need to know the weather, I can still update you, because I'm sitting next to an open window. It's drizzling, the winds are calm, and it's mild and a bit humid. All is quiet except for the birds singing. It's a beautiful day. Let's actually go out and be aware of it instead of checking to see how it will change throughout the day or week. We can use the extra time we have to be more fit, more creative, more alive. Mama Bear would be proud!

> "How does God's love abide in anyone who has the world's goods and sees a brother or sister in need and yet refuses help?"
>
> 1 John 3:17

Rich Man, Poor Man

I watched a documentary a few days ago about the exodus of boys from Sudan in the 1980s and 1990s. It was a fascinating look at a culture suffering from horrific poverty, war, and disease, surrounded by nothing but death. They walked over a thousand miles, across three countries, in the sweltering desert with no shoes, no parents, and no direction. Tens of thousands died, and tens of thousands remained, only to endure unimaginable hardships. After years of such living, a small number of these "lost boys" were flown to the United States and set up with apartments for three months until they could obtain employment. They had never seen electricity, running water, plumbing, etc. Yet after only several months in the United States, they said that life in this country "is hard."

Please let that sink in. These young men walked over a thousand miles over the course of a few years. They were barefoot with no food, no medicine, no clothes, no parents, no direction, and no future. Enemies and wild animals attacked them. They suffered from disease, starvation, and dehydration, and yet they said that life in the USA "is hard."

Though they roomed together in the U.S. in groups of three or four, they said that they were lonely, and they greatly missed their friends back home. They were confused at a culture where the long days are spent working for money and little time is spent with family, where the food cannot be traced to its original source, where Christmas is spent worshipping someone named Santa, where the people do not speak to each other much less support each other, and where the clothes, homes, and automobiles somehow define one's character.

The change in the young men could be seen almost immediately upon boarding the plane in Africa. It was a transition visible in their eyes, the windows to their very souls, from sensitive human beings to complex robots in a bustling society of machines, money, and mayhem. They went from simple survival strategies to complexities and confusion everywhere, beginning at the very floors under their feet to disturbing visual stimulation being thrown at them in every direction. You would have thought that they would have come here and praised God. Instead, they were sad, confused, and lonely. If that doesn't wake us up, nothing will.

It really hit home for me this morning as I got into my car at 6:30 a.m. and pulled into the Dunkin' Donuts drive-through. I placed an order from my car speaking to a machine, took my Styrofoam cup, and drove in my vehicle down the highway alone. My day continued to be monopolized by one machine after another with very little real interaction with another human being. I found myself thinking of the African boys hanging out together with their clans back home, swimming in the Nile, walking to get water and food, and laughing, playing, and helping each other. I felt like a lonely robot.

For a rich country, we are indeed quite poor.

> *"Jesus said to him,*
> *'If you wish to be perfect, go,*
> *sell your possessions,*
> *and give the money to the poor,*
> *and you will have treasure in heaven;*
> *then come, follow me.'"*
>
> **Matthew 19:21**

"Blessed are those who hunger and thirst for righteousness, for they will be filled."

Matthew 5:6

Hunger Pangs

I remember a particularly gloomy day a few years ago. The temperature was a bit cool, and it was dark and overcast. My mood apparently decreased along with the sunshine, so what did I do? I went shopping.

This was a fairly new thing for me. I normally stay far away from the stores, but I had lately found myself shopping to try to kill time and/or to pacify myself. I only spent about an hour and less than eighty dollars on eight items of clothing for myself and my husband, but the moment I started to check out, I felt sick to my stomach. It wasn't that I couldn't afford it; it's just that I have a persistent voice in my head that repeatedly questions me: "Is it a need or want?"

To make matters worse, as I left the shopping center parking lot and started driving towards the highway, a man was standing at a stoplight with a sign that read something to the effect of "Hungry, will work for food." As I glanced his way, I inadvertently caught direct eye contact with him. It was such an awkward moment as I sat staring at him from the comfort of my car with my needless new purchases in the back seat. His gaze was sincere, and I quickly looked the other way and prayed for the light to turn green. Once I finally started driving again, I began making up excuses in my mind, such as "He's probably looking for money to buy drugs or alcohol. I wouldn't have been helping him at all. It would have been enabling." Really though, who am I to judge these things?

So there I sat with a few more dresses, and my husband had several more of those golf shirts. (He doesn't golf, but apparently there isn't a fashion designer on earth who can come up with another style of shirt for men). The look in the man's eyes stuck in my mind. Imagine what that eighty dollars might have done for him.

Perhaps he was just an example of all of those individuals out there to whom eighty dollars would have meant much more than another shirt or dress. It might have purchased a week's worth of groceries. I personally know friends who could have used that money.

The next day, I went back to that store to return everything. If I did so and simply returned the money to my checking account, it probably wouldn't even be noticed. However, if I took the money and sent it to someone else, or purchased a gas card or supermarket gift card for that person or several people, imagine the joy, relief, and hope it would cause. Instead of ending my day with a feeling of guilt and emptiness, I could end the day knowing that I made a difference. Unlike shopping, this idea feels natural and thoroughly gratifying. I just have to break the cycle of consumerism and stop getting sucked into the ideas of a materialistic society.

I'm so glad that God placed that man in my midst because I ignored the subtler internal signal when I was at the checkout line. I truly believe that God's law is "written within my heart" (Psalm 40:8). I found an interesting translation that better fits my experience from the Aramaic Bible in Plain English: "To do your pleasure oh, God, I have desired, and your Law is within my belly." No wonder I was sick to my stomach!

Today I will remember and act upon Jesus' words: "It is more blessed to give than to receive" (Acts 20:35). I have no doubt that my stomach and heart will be pleased.

"Give, and it will be given to you. A good measure, pressed down, shaken together, running over, will be put into your lap; for the measure you give will be the measure you get back."

Luke 6:38

"Nor will they say,
'Look, here it is!'
or 'There it is!'
For, in fact,
the kingdom of God
is within you."

Luke 17:21

Look Within

I'd been going to physical therapy for a while for minor back problems. They'd been putting me on several machines that stretched my spine to expand the shortening spaces in my aging discs. As I lay there, I could hear the conversations of the people around me, most of them elderly and in pain. One morning was more depressing than usual. Two women were discussing their pain, their lives, their children, and their grandchildren. The conversation went something like this:

Woman 1: "Geez, you finally get to an age where you have time and money to enjoy things, but you can't enjoy anything because your body is falling apart."
Woman 2: "Yeah, things sure were different when we were young."
Woman 1: "I'm all by myself. My husband died last year. My kids never come around. They are too busy.

At this point, the physical therapist enters with yet another elderly person, this one a man. Their conversation began about how he got his injury from golfing:

Man 1: "I'd like to get back on the golf course soon. I'm retired, and you know, when you're retired, there's really not much to do."
P.T.: "I know, my father-in-law golfs. Since he retired, he golfs about three to five days a week."
Man 1: Yeah, there's really nothing else to do. You know, you're not working anymore, so it's great to get out and keep

busy hitting some balls. I worked hard all those years, so now it's time to just relax."

So what's it all about? Are we here to work hard to support our families and then spend the last twenty years or so of life hanging out on a golf course or in a shopping mall? Are we here to raise our children to expect them to provide us with friendship and security? Are we here to earn money to save so that we can live comfortably in a beachfront condo?

I think we've worked hard for all the wrong reasons. I think we've let our society dictate our truth, which is really no truth at all. Yet, I think that we still possess within us everything we need to fulfill us beyond our imaginations.

Luke 10:27 reads: "You shall love the Lord your God with all your heart, with all your soul, with all your strength, and with all your mind; and your neighbor as yourself." God first, then self, then others. It makes perfect sense, but we are all mixed up. We expect our jobs, our families, or our friends to fill us. When we lose them, we expect other "things" to do the trick. Then we often think we have nothing to give others because nobody is giving anything to us.

Yet the answer has been the same for all eternity. It is the reason for our existence, and until we look within, we will remain bitter, angry, lonely, and unfulfilled. Imagine the possibilities (and I don't mean a hole in one!)! The Kingdom of God is within you! What will you do with that knowledge today?

*"The eyes of all look to you,
and you give them their food in due season.
You open your hand,
satisfying the desire of every living thing."*

Psalm 145:15-16

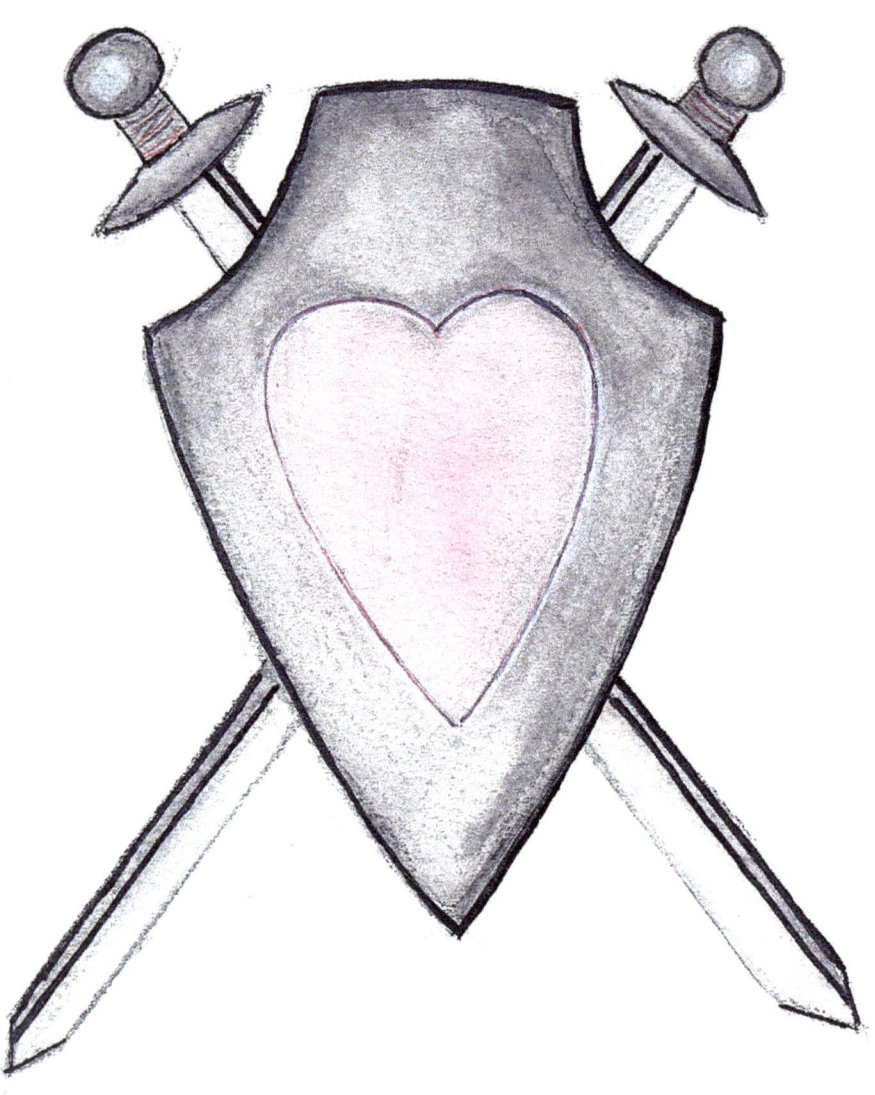

The Whole Armor of God

Ephesians 6:10-20

A Knight in Shining Armor

My husband and I celebrated our twenty-ninth wedding anniversary last month. We are still in love. My eldest daughter looks at us as if we couldn't possibly be for real. It's a whole new world she's living in, and it's no fairy tale, at least not the happily-ever-after kind. I'm no prude (well maybe a little), but the things that are going on these days make me sick, sad, and confused. How did such basic, primal behavior go so drastically wrong?

It's really not meant to be this complicated. It's fundamental. It's the birds and the bees for goodness' sake! Guy meets girl. The two feel a chemistry. Guy pursues girl. Girl knows she's got the goods, and she knows how to dangle the carrot to keep him interested. Guy chases the carrot like the hungry little rabbit that he is, using every resource he has to win his prize. Girl waits for him to prove his intentions. Everyone wins in the end.

Here's a quick version of what today's rabbit chase looks like. Girl is desperate for guy. Girl will do anything to get guy. Guy knows that and does absolutely nothing to pursue girl. Well, if the girl is lucky, she'll get a lame text message. If a miracle happens, they might go on some semblance of a date. The girl will pay, or they will split the bill. They have sex. Guy doesn't text anymore. Girl doesn't understand why. Round two...three...four...five...six...on and on it goes. Nobody wins. Nobody knows why.

Maybe the calamity has something to do with the modern pace of life: immediate gratification. Maybe it has to do with television, computers, and every other technology. I'm not here to speculate on the cause, just to attest to the truth. It involves listening to that voice within that tells you right from wrong, good from evil. It concerns such antiquated things as faith, tradition, and love. It has something to do with purity, integrity, honesty, and commitment.

I'm not making this stuff up. The Church has it all spelled out for us as the seven heavenly virtues: chastity, temperance, charity, diligence, patience, kindness, and humility. Their corresponding vices are lust, gluttony, greed, sloth, wrath, envy, and pride. It's all right there, the solutions and problems. None of it is simple though. It never was. It's a spiritual war, and it's in full swing.

In Ephesians 6:11, St. Paul showed us the way to be victorious in this war. He said:

> *"Put on the whole armor of God,*
> *so that you may be able*
> *to stand against*
> *the wiles of the devil."*

I know chastity belts are obsolete, but I also know that God's armor is still very much alive. Good fairy tales usually involve a knight in shining armor. So if you want the fairy tale, suit up.

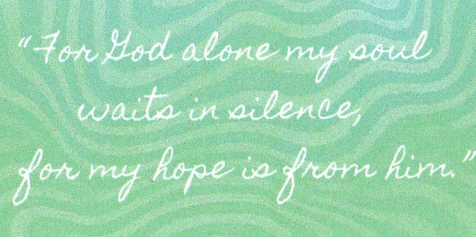

"For God alone my soul waits in silence, for my hope is from him."

Psalm 62:5

The Remedy for Misery

I went to see *Les Miserables* in theaters twice. I was so moved and inspired by this movie that I could probably write a blog a day for the next month based solely on the messages I received from it. I sat up close and felt the energy of the human spirit as it confronts love, war, loneliness, fear, joy, pain, rejection, protection, forgiveness, blame, shame, purity, perversion, and everything else in between life and death.

Best of all, it was all relational. The most beautiful, poignant and painful moments in the movie (and in life) occur through the impact of one person to another and the trickle-down effect that follows. We affect each other for better or worse by the choices that we make and the actions – or inaction – that result from those choices.

In one scene in *Les Miserables*, a desperate man steals a bunch of silver from a priest. Instead of turning him over to the police, the priest offers the thief more silver and tells him to use it to start a new life. This act of kindness so moves the thief that he feels the spirit of love (probably for the first time in a long time), and that love transforms him. He is a changed man, and he lives a new life with dignity and compassion. He goes on to influence and transform other lives, none of which could have happened without the decision that the priest made. That one choice, made in an instant, could very easily and justifiably have been to report the man to the police. Who would have blamed him? He didn't have time to predict what his decision might mean; he simply chose to love and not judge or condemn.

Every one of us and every single person we encounter is influenced and transformed for better or worse through each and every experience we have with one another. We may be perfectly justified in our decisions to persecute for an action against our loved ones, or ourselves, but we must be mindful when making our decisions. Each choice absolutely will result in some future consequence, and that will continue like a rolling stone picking up or shattering particles along the way. We will probably never know the full ramifications until we reach our final destination. Sometimes we can mend the wounds, but most remain hidden or neglected. As with any injury, prevention is the best practice. In general, it is less costly and much easier to prevent a wound than it is to heal one. Wounded souls are no exception.

Interestingly, there was a strong spiritual aspect to the movie, and the initiator of the first source of loving healing was a priest. His sense of peace, love, and wholeness was obvious, and it was from that peace that he could give. That comes from God. Period.

If we are seeking to be filled by other people, places, or things, it's simply not going to happen. We cannot feed our spirit with something physical. Have you ever tried nourishing your physical body with spiritual food? You would starve and die. The same thing happens to our spirit when we try to feed it with physical stuff (people, places, or things). We gradually starve our spirit, and it eventually dies.

I would say that all of our relationship issues are spiritual issues. We are seeking from others who are present to us physically something that our spirits need. Occasionally, we may be lucky enough to meet someone who feeds his spirit and can share with us the fruits of that nourishment, but it is not the physical person who is then feeding us. It is the spirit within. That spirit can change the world.

We live in a society and an era of instant gratification. If I can't get it on the computer, the phone, or the television right here and right now, then I'm moving on to the next thing that can give it to me. This mentality doesn't fly in the spiritual realm, and as a result, we are a society of spiritually sick people acting and reacting in ways that hurt each other terribly. It's an unhealthy and persistent cycle that will continue until each of us takes the time to nourish our spirit. It doesn't cost a thing. It's easy, safe, and extremely effective. All we have to do is set time aside to be still.

"For you yourselves know very well
that the day of the Lord
will come like a thief in the night.
When they say, 'There is peace and security,'
then sudden destruction will come upon them,
as labor pains come upon a pregnant woman,
and there will be no escape!"

1 Thessalonians 5:2-3

Live Deliberately

As I peacefully drove along the Appalachian Trail yesterday, an ambulance raced past me with its siren blaring. I wondered who was inside the vehicle and about their situation. To be honest, most of the time, I don't consider the person inside. Someone once told me that they say a prayer each time an ambulance passes by. That's a nice thought, but honestly, I normally pray that there isn't an accident up ahead that will hold me up. This time, however, I somehow felt a strong sense of urgency, and it made me realize how quickly life can change.

Some years back, my daughter (then eleven years old) and I met my husband for dinner on his way home from work. My daughter ordered one of the daily specials that the waitress announced (without offering the price). I think it was lobster, and it ended up costing a lot more than we would have normally spent. She couldn't eat even half of the large meal, so we carried most of it home in the back seat of my car, where my daughter happily sat with a full belly and her favorite book. We followed behind my husband's vehicle on the 15-minute drive home in the pouring rain. It was another one of those days that we all take for granted: uneventful and ordinary.

Less than halfway, home the rain started really coming down, though nothing that I hadn't experienced before. I am a cautious driver, so I slowed down to about forty-five miles per hour, and I put my SUV in four-wheel drive just to be safe. I glanced in the rearview mirror to the back seat, where my daughter was wearing her seat belt and still reading. Up ahead, my husband seemed to be handling his own. Suddenly, out of nowhere, a vision appeared that is forever etched in my mind. Two large vehicles (an SUV and a van) appeared nose-to-nose across the width of my side of the highway, swirling at me at an incredible rate of speed. In the time that I could say "WHAT THE ...," it was over.

The next thing I remember is waking up to the sound of someone knocking on my window asking if I was okay. I couldn't believe it; I was alive! My daughter was hysterically screaming in the back seat, so I knew she too was alive. We were taken out of the car and sent to the side of the road, where we sat in shock in the pounding rain. To my left was the van, which had crashed into the side of the mountain. The driver was still unconscious with her head in the steering wheel. In front of me were my car and the other SUV. There were car parts, glass, and debris strewn about the highway like litter tossed from a dump truck.

My daughter (still screaming) remembered that my husband was ahead of us and became even more hysterical, because she was afraid he was involved too. At the same time, he was realizing that there were suddenly no cars behind him on the highway, and he knew something was drastically wrong. He turned around and drove north in the southbound lanes only to arrive at the scene of a horrific accident. What a beautiful moment it was when we were safely reunited. My husband sheltered us from the rain in his vehicle as he went to help the other victims. The ambulances began showing up on the scene; cars began backing up for miles in both directions; and my daughter and I began coming back to the reality of the whole thing.

I felt helpless, powerless, and small, and all I could do that meant anything at all was to pray. So my daughter and I prayed aloud together. That wasn't something that we would normally do back then, but there was nothing else to do at that point other than to thank God we survived and to pray for the others. I sat motionless, knowing that my life could have ended right there. I was given the real awareness of how quickly life can end, and I knew some things had to change. At that time, I had been spending a lot of time on a business that I ran from home. Actually, the business ran me, and as I sat there, I realized how ridiculously meaningless it all was. Very few things in life have real meaning when death is imminent.

My daughter and I ended up with injuries that would heal in time, as did several of the other victims. The unconscious woman that I saw in the van died that day, probably just driving home like we were. That's how quickly life can change or end: in an instant, without warning, and "like a thief in the night."

We all know this, but we don't live that way. We live with the expectancy of another day, another moment, another meal, like the one we had prior to the accident (the remains of which ended up along with my demolished vehicle at the junkyard).

I've said before that I believe we live our best lives in the constant awareness of death. That might sound morbid to some, but it is often not until we have a brush with death that we really start living. Otherwise, we continue doing that which we really don't want to do (thinking it will change in time), or we wait for a future that may never come.

One of my favorite quotes has always been this one by Henry David Thoreau: "I went to the woods because I wished to live deliberately, to front only the essential facts of life, and see if I could not learn what it had to teach, and not, when I came to die, discover that I have not lived."

Let's live our lives *deliberately* right now. This moment is all we have and can be our last with the blink of an eye.

> *"For we know only in part,*
> *and we prophesy only in part;*
> *but when the complete comes,*
> *the partial will come to an end."*
>
> **1 Corinthians 13:9-10**

Living and Learning

Here's a heck of a revelation: Perhaps I am not as smart as I think I am. It could be that I do not have all the answers. Conceivably, my opinion is not the only opinion. Maybe, just maybe, there are other viewpoints, and they actually have value.

Did you ever feel so strongly about something that you were certain you were right? Did you feel justified in stating your opinion because it was all in the name of righteousness?

It reminds me of the inspector/officer in *Les Miserables* who was chasing the thief for years, making the guy's life a living hell. The inspector (named Javert) is really not a bad guy at all. Technically he's just fighting for justice. However, he is so blinded by his own self-righteousness that he doesn't see the big picture. Sure, Valjean (the thief) stole some bread and broke his parole, but the guy was just trying to feed his sister's children who were poor and hungry. Was that a crime or an act of love? Valjean repented, and he spent the rest of his life spreading his wealth and love with all those around him.

Javert couldn't see that because he was so focused on himself and his mission of "justice." He wasted his life persecuting a good man.

Soon after viewing *Les Miserables* for the first time, I was in my contemporary art history class getting more and more perturbed at the paintings I was viewing. I am not a fan of contemporary art, and being an artist myself, I thought I surely know what art is and what is not. The philosophical jargon that I was reading in the textbooks was frustrating and angering me. I was completely certain that my viewpoint was correct, and everyone else was just trying to shove nonsense down my throat. I'm right, I thought, in defending "true" art. Why should I be taught such rubbish? At the end of the class, the professor told us to "keep an open mind." I'm certain she was speaking to me and speak to me she did.

I never thought of myself as being closed-minded. I'm as open-minded as the next person to things that seem reasonable and sensible to me! That pretty much fits the definition of closed-minded: "having a mind firmly unreceptive to new ideas or arguments." Guess what the synonyms are: "inflexible, obstinate, pigheaded, rigid." Ouch.

St. Paul reminds me to "clothe [myself] with compassion, kindness, humility, gentleness and patience" (Colossians 3:12). An old friend of mine used to say that humility is "being teachable." I certainly cannot be teachable with a closed mind. Today I will try to walk gently, patiently, and to keep an open mind, which will lead me to become a kinder and humbler person, not to mention a lot less frustrated!

"Do nothing from selfish ambition or conceit, but in humility regard others as better than yourselves. Let each of you look not to your own interests, but to the interests of others. Let the same mind be in you that was in Christ Jesus."

Philippians 2:3-5

"Create in me a clean heart, O God,
and put a new and right
spirit within me."

Psalm 51:10

Enduring the Chore of Change

After almost thirteen years of living with the same decor in my house, I suddenly decided one day that it was (in the infamous words of Bill Clinton) "time for a change." The dark-colored paint and old-fashioned wallpaper no longer pleased me. In fact, they downright depressed me. So one day, I started ripping away at the paper. The top layer peeled off easier than I expected, but what remained was a layer of thin paper stuck to the wall by a stubborn glue. I had to use a remover to get rid of that final layer, and all of this got me thinking about change.

It would have been easier to just leave the room as it was than to go through the work of making the alteration. It required time and effort that I would have rather devoted to something more pleasurable. Sure, I could have just kept running in and out of the house rather than stopping to really observe my surroundings, but I decided it was time for a change. I had to take on the mentality that if I'm going to do it right, it's going to take time, patience, and a lot of elbow grease. After the first layer was off, I wouldn't have dreamed of stopping, because if I didn't go through the nitty gritty work of scraping off the stubborn paper and residual glue, the end result would be much less attractive. It will not emanate its full elegance.

When it comes to changes within me, I'm much more likely to stop peeling after the first layer. It's too much work to go deeper, and it's a lot easier to hide than the wallpaper. I can keep myself busy and running in many activities and directions to avoid looking within. I can even doctor myself up in all kinds of ways to hide that residual stuff, and nobody will be any worse for the wear, right?

The wallpaper has taught me a lesson. If I want my end result to be beautiful and to emanate that beauty, I must do the work to remove the underlying stuff. It's going to be a chore, but how can I even think about leaving it as is? I want my life to bless and grace far beyond what I expect of the four walls in my home. I must remember to give myself the same time and energy. It might be difficult, but the blessings will far outweigh the hardships. Hopefully I'll do this more frequently than every thirteen years, though!

> *"For dreams come with many cares,
> and a fool's voice with many words."*
>
> **Ecclesiastes 5:3**

A Girl Can Dream, Can't She?

Martin Luther King Day always gets me thinking about the man with a dream. Imagine a world without such people, a world filled with people who are either too cynical, fearful, tired, busy, or just plain shallow to dream. Unfortunately, I think those people are the majority.

My dad had lots of dreams; he talked about them all the time. He wanted to live in (or even just travel to) Oregon, Montana, or Wyoming. Every few years, the location moved a little to the west or east. For some reason, however (usually financial), he just laughed when asked about actually pursuing his dreams. Dreams, he seemed to think, were for dreamers, and he was a realist. He had a wife and four kids to feed, a home to maintain, and sometimes three jobs. Dreams? Bah, humbug!

Maybe there's a stigma behind the word itself. It seems to imply a fantasy, something foolish or impossible that's not meant to be taken seriously. You know what they say: there are the dreamers and then there are the doers, as if you can only be one or the other.

What's ironic is the greatest doers had to start with a dream. Harriet Tubman said, "Every great dream begins with a dreamer. Always remember, you have within you the strength, the patience, and the passion to reach for the stars to change the world."

For the sake of semantics and the realists out there, let's change the word to "vision." Do you have a vision for your life? Do you have a vision for the world, and what is your role in that vision? What are you doing to achieve it? I've got so many visions; I don't know where to start! I have to be honest though – people don't make it easy for me to have a vision. They seem to try their best to deflate my dream balloon rather than using that energy to inflate their own.

I graduated college at the age of 51. It's a vision I'd had for a long time and one that I didn't begin until an unconventional age. At that time, most people were supportive. When my graduation from undergrad was imminent, I decided to continue on to grad school. Several people then asked me why on earth I am pursuing all this education. "What do you plan to do with it? Why are you spending all that money? Why does your husband tolerate you? (Yes someone asked that!) Are you going to start a career at age 60? Why would you start working at an age when most people are retiring?"

Let me set the record straight right now: I want to change the world, and I personally do not feel that I can accomplish that without being properly educated! Harriet Tubman told me it's okay! Now can we move on and be productive?

The world is not an easy place, but I can guarantee you that it improves greatly with each person who sets on a path to pursue a great dream. Move in the direction of something good, something beautiful, or something inspirational. Take some time to listen to that inner voice, and then follow your heart. Stick with people who are going to support you. If you don't know where to start, drop me a note and I'll help you figure it out!

I truly believe with all my heart that anything is possible. You just have to begin. So begin right now.

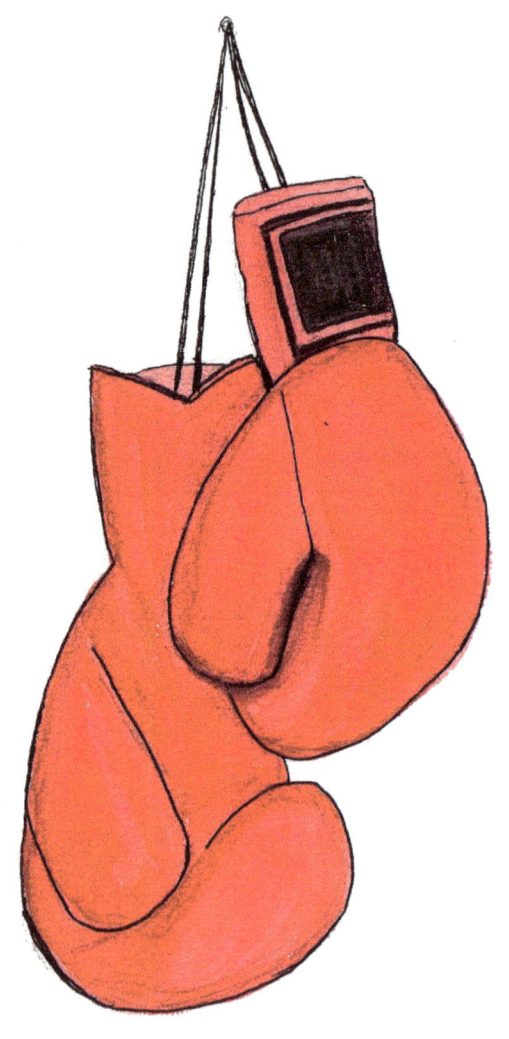

"I have fought the good fight,
I have finished the race,
I have kept the faith."

2 Timothy 4:7

The Fight of Your Life

Have you heard the song "Life's A Dance?" The chorus proclaims: "Life's a dance you learn as you go; Sometimes you lead, sometimes you follow; Don't worry about what you don't know; Life's a dance you learn as you go." I like the song just fine, but most of the time I wouldn't describe life as a dance. I envision a dance as enjoyable, exhilarating, and rhythmic. It's pretty and graceful. A good dancer always hears the beat and keeps in step with it. It's fun, and it flows. I don't know about you, but that doesn't sound like my life!

I think I would describe life as a good fight – you know, like Rocky. I'm in the ring, and I'm fighting. Some rounds I'm on top, and I feel like I can fight forever. Look out world, here I come!

Other times, I'm getting my butt kicked. The world just keeps punching and swinging, and I can't seem to punch back. I'm tired, and I can just barely hold on. Those are the times I wish the darn bell would ring and give me a break. Wouldn't it be nice if that happened? Then I could sit down in the corner where that guy would wipe me down and, in a calm, supportive, but firm manner, whisper encouraging words and instructions in my ear.

If life's a fight, then we need to train like boxers. Otherwise, we won't have the strength, agility, or stamina to endure. Then we'll either avoid the fight or go into it timidly and expecting failure.

Rocky was just a bum in the ring swinging for some cash. He didn't take it too seriously at first. He had some crude physical strength going on, enough to get him in the ring, but he didn't really train for the fight at first. It was tough, and the payout reflected his lack of training. Then he was asked to fight a champion. Suddenly, he had to take the game seriously, or he was going to look like a fool on national television.

Queue in the Rocky that we remember – stretching, drinking raw eggs, running night and day, beating up slabs of meat, working out in the gym, doing one-arm pushups, listening to the advice of his trainers, and finally running the steps of the Philadelphia Museum of Art. He trained hard, but that wasn't all he needed. He was given a dog to keep him company when he went out running. He had a good manager to direct him, and he had the loving support and encouragement of friends and his community. Let's not forget that he had some pretty good inspirational music to boot!

Life is no different. We need a good manager to direct us. (Mine directs me through prayer.) We need company, support, and encouragement. We absolutely must train, including exercise and eating healthy foods. We must prepare our minds as well as our bodies. The two cannot be separated because the fight requires both mental and physical strength and agility. We have to take it all seriously and not just be bums in the ring.

Let's wake up each day to prepare for the ring. We'll train hard by exercising our bodies and minds. We'll consult with our "manager," take others with us if we get bored and lonely, and invoke the support of our family, friends, and community. Don't forget a corner man. All are needed if we want to succeed and be able to say, along with St. Paul, "I have fought the good fight, I have finished the race, I have kept the faith." (2 Timothy 4:7)

And what the heck, turn on the Rocky theme song if you need some extra inspiration! Whatever you do, just don't throw in the towel.

"Do you not know that in a race the runners all compete, but only one receives the prize? Run in such a way that you may win it."

1 Corinthians 9:24

"Come to me, all you that are weary
and are carrying heavy burdens,
and I will give you rest.
Take my yoke upon you,
and learn from me;
for I am gentle and humble in heart,
and you will find rest for your souls.
For my yoke is easy,
and my burden is light."

Matthew 11:28-30

Are You Gonna Carry That Weight?

I remember my mom singing around the house when I was a child. Oh, believe me, she wasn't feeling so joyful that she couldn't contain herself. It wasn't a cheerful humming, but rather a sad, lamenting moan. The lyrics were always the same: "Make the world go away and get it off my shoulders . . ." (by Eddy Arnold). I'm not a fan of the song, but I find myself humming that when I have been carrying around burdens that are really weighing me down.

Sometimes it seems as though it would be much easier to carry a fifty-pound suitcase around the entire day than it is to carry those things that have no physical weight at all. Things like fear, anger, sadness, frustration, blame, regret, and shame put more pressure on my body, mind, and soul than would the suitcase. These invisible disturbances become as substantial as my mind will allow them to be.

If there's one thing I'm good at lately, it's turning thin air into concrete heavy enough to crush me. It can get overwhelming, exhausting, and downright frightening trying to hold the weight of all that pressure.

It occurred to me one night that I don't have to lug the world around on my shoulders. I can take it off and put it down. Better yet, I don't have to pick it up to begin with.

Have you ever had days where your cell phone just won't stop? As I'm on the phone dealing with one crisis, a text comes through. While responding to the text, an email popped up. Each situation stresses me to the max, and I actually think for a moment of throwing the phone violently out the window. How much simpler it would have been to simply shut the phone off and take the world off my shoulders, for a moment, an hour, or God forbid the entire night!

I have to remind myself constantly that I have a choice. All I had to do was to turn the phone off and put it away. I can choose to be harried, angry, and frightened, or I can make a decision to take those traits off and put them down. It truly is that simple in nearly any situation. It's much easier to carry around patience, courage, and compatibility, and they don't seem to weigh an ounce! In fact, those attributes have the opposite effect; they lift you up and make you feel lighter.

What do you choose to carry with you today?

*"Cast your burden on the Lord,
and he will sustain you;
he will never permit
the righteous to be moved."*

Psalm 55:22

"God said, 'See, I have given you every plant yielding seed that is upon the face of all the earth, and every tree with seed in its fruit; you shall have them for food.'"

Genesis 1:29

How Does Your Garden Grow?

Every year at this time I think about growing a vegetable garden, though I rarely follow through. I've done this in the past when the kids were small to save money and teach them the process. At that time, I purchased the small vegetable plants and transplanted them in my garden. I always thought that was kind of silly, but that's what most people seemed to do. I thought if I wanted to grow vegetables from seeds that I had to plant the seeds in small containers in the house weeks in advance, and then transplant them into the garden at the right time. (Hey, when I grew up, we had a concrete backyard. What did I know about this stuff?)

A few years ago, I decided to throw all caution to the wind, and I planted the seeds right in the garden. Of course, in my mind, it couldn't possibly be that simple. I first had to rent a tiller to turn the old soil. I made little rock pathways to walk on so that I wouldn't crush the seeds/plants. I reinforced the fencing to keep critters out, and I think I added manure to the soil and a cute little garden angel decoration. Then came the doubtful part. I opened the first package of seeds, and they were so tiny they could blow away with the slightest breeze. I couldn't imagine that a plant could grow from one seed, so I planted about five or six seeds in each tiny hole, all the while thinking there was no way this was going to work.

Anyway, lo and behold it didn't take long or any additional work on my part before little green shoots started sprouting from the soil! It felt like a miracle! It's the simple things that we take for granted. I put this miniscule, almost microscopic, seed in dirt, and a luscious vegetable plant was growing to nourish me. I began to get excited, and I started really caring for the garden. I weeded it frequently, and I watered it (probably too frequently). I was fascinated that I could grow real food from inexpensive, tiny seeds in my own backyard!

As I continued watching the plants grow and the interactions of the insects, animals, invading weeds, weather, and myself, I began to realize that within this small backyard garden, I could possibly find the answer to many of life's mysteries. I'm sure it is no coincidence that the Creation story took place in a garden and that God created seed-bearing plants. Genesis 1:11 reads: "Then God said, 'Let the earth put forth vegetation: plants yielding seed, and fruit trees of every kind on earth that bear fruit with the seed in it.'" Seeds are amazing!

We humans tend to complicate things way more than we need to. I really believe that most things are just plain simple. God has it all worked out, yet we try to manipulate and complicate matters. At the same time, we tend to overlook the beautiful complexities in the simple things like seeds. A seed is a miracle! Modern conveniences are supposed to be adding quality to our lives, but truly we are missing out on so much by not working in the garden.

Let's plant some seeds today, and let's see what nourishment the garden has to bestow upon us. If we're looking and listening, I have a feeling it's going to produce food not only for our stomachs, but for our minds, hearts, and souls as well.

> *"Do not be overcome by evil,
> but overcome evil with good."*
>
> **Romans 12:21**

It's Black or White

I once painted a picture of a guy balancing between two worlds: good and evil. One of my professors asked something like, "Is there nothing in between? The guy's gonna either fall into heaven or hell?" Ha! Good question for today's society, which rarely considers either to be a reality. Maybe I'll have to paint a new one that might resonate more clearly, but it's not going to be easy, because society is convinced that anything goes, and there are no consequences. What is the line that divides good and evil? If you can't envision that, then surely we can all agree that there is a line that divides right and wrong. Can't we?

Do you see a clear line between what is right and what is wrong? Is that even important anymore? You might be amazed at how many people dismiss the Ten Commandments as an archaic set of rules that simply don't apply to today's culture. We're certainly seeing the effects of that dismissal.

So where do you turn to discover (without a doubt) what is right and what is wrong? Dr. Phil? Oprah? A friend? It's something to think about, because if we are not clear or concerned about right and wrong, then we're living in a state of meaninglessness. We're feeling the pain of it.

I paint a lot of black and white paintings. So my professor may well have asked: "Is there nothing in between black and white?" Sure, there are gray areas, and they are just that, fuzzy, vague areas that do not offer any type of clarity.

I hate to be the one to break it to you, but there is black and there is white. There is good and there is evil. There is truth and there are lies. There is light and there is darkness. It takes effort to be on either side, and none of it is easy. In fact, it seems to get harder every day. However, I believe with all my heart that "the good side" is worth fighting for. I don't want to live in a world of darkness, of gray areas and evil. I want to live in the light. It's not easy, but it's worth the struggle. We need direction; we need community; we need to stick together to fight the good fight (1 Timothy 6:12).

*"O send out your light and your truth;
let them lead me;
let them bring me to your holy hill
and to your dwelling."*

Psalm 43:3

"But ask the animals,
and they will teach you;
the birds of the air,
and they will tell you;
ask the plants of the earth,
and they will teach you;
and the fish of the sea
will declare to you.
Who among all these does not know
that the hand of the Lord
has done this?"

Job 12:7-9

The Inconvenient Truth

My eldest daughter called me one night. At the time, she was out west in Washington at a camp north of Seattle training for an internship. Before she left, we checked online to see what type of facilities were at the camp. It looked beautiful, and the cabins appeared rather modern. When she arrived there, she discovered her "cabin" was just a very small lean-to. To add to the discomfort, there was no electricity.

I hadn't heard much from her on a daily basis. There was the problem of the time difference, there was also very poor cellular reception, and she was working twelve hours a day. When I finally got to hear her voice, I realized that I hadn't heard her that happy in a long time. She said that she couldn't understand or explain it. She was sleeping in a shack with no walls; it was cold and raining most of the time; she was with a bunch of strangers; and she was working long, hard days... yet she had no stress, she was sleeping wonderfully, and she was content.

When my daughter left for the trip, she left behind all the modern conveniences of her daily life. At the same time, she left behind a ridiculously hectic pace of living, and a society that focuses on self-gratification at any cost. She went from activity to activity, job to job, state to state seeking something that would help her to feel a sense of purpose. Yet all of the modern conveniences, the excessive privileges, and indulgent activities left her feeling anxious, even angry, and quite unfulfilled. Now she was back to the basics of living (less than basic, one might argue), and she was stress-free and content.

I've experienced what my daughter was experiencing, even if to a lesser degree. I've been without power for a few hours, forgot my cell phone at home for an entire day, or perhaps been without a car for a few days. Somehow those experiences are always kind of freeing. I am forced to slow down, simplify, and make the best of the moment. I seem to have the innate ability to make something out of nothing: to find light in the darkness (when without power), to create warmth, to keep busy and productive even without technology. Somehow, I instinctively know that I am not created to live in this complex environment.

My spiritual director once told me that we are "human beings becoming." Modernity seems to convince us that we are human beings becoming wiser and savvier, but at the same time, we are left feeling rather unengaged with ourselves and our world. It's not natural, and we are of the natural world. I think we just need to be human beings becoming human beings again. Perhaps the trick is to use our modern conveniences at our own convenience, to control them so they don't control us. We have to routinely remove ourselves from the busyness and enter a place of simplicity and nature. I think we'll discover that we can be human beings becoming truly aware, alive, and whole again, without feeling inconvenienced at all.

The following was written by my daughter Mia while away at the camp:

It's crazy how fast you get used to things. Two more nights and I won't be able to fall asleep to a banjo, guitar, and a medley of voices singing folk songs into the cool night air. I won't hear the rain falling steadily onto the roof of my tiny, open-air cabin that I share with three girls I met only a week ago. I won't wake up with the sun (if we're lucky) extending its morning rays like arms through moss-covered trees. I won't grab my towel from an overhanging beam and tread to the communal bathroom to take a shower that's never completely warm but tolerable enough to jump in, scrub, and jump out. I won't arrive at every meal to the same faces, smells (some not too great), and chaotic clamor for coffee in an attempt to grab some before it's all gone. I won't go to sleep curled in the fetal position, wearing two pairs of socks and sleeping bag pulled completely over my head in an attempt to keep out the cold as the temperature dips below 40. I will have my own room, privacy, electricity, doors, windows, heat, air conditioning, a fridge, my car, grocery stores, freedom to come and go anywhere, anytime, a computer with internet, and an entire closet in place of a duffel bag. I'll be able to join a gym, drink a beer, go to a movie, make phone calls, straighten my hair, wear heels, and sleep in a bed with two memory foam pillows and 300 thread count sheets. Somehow it just doesn't seem like a fair trade.

"I want their hearts to be
encouraged and united in love,
so that they may have
all the riches of assured understanding
and have the knowledge of God's mystery,
that is, Christ himself,
in whom are hidden all the treasures of
wisdom and knowledge."

Colossians 2:2-3

Who Knows?

One day, I was eating an organic, grass-fed steak for lunch, which led me to wonder how on earth I knew for sure that this meat is organic. I was trusting that the company that processes and packages the stuff was honest and doing the right thing. Not only did I pay more money for this kind of beef, but I did so believing that I would be less at risk of E-coli and not subjected to ingesting unnecessary hormones. I had no idea where all of this happens. I'll never see the farm where the cows are happily eating beautiful green, untreated grass. I buy and consume this in complete trust.

My lunch got me thinking about all of the other situations in my life that call for my trust in (for all intents and purposes) invisible powers. I trust that the gas companies really need to charge close to $4.00 per gallon (I think I just choked on my steak!). I trust that the orange juice is really made from oranges. I trust that the charities I give to are utilizing the money wisely. I trust that the "Under 550" meals at Applebee's really do have less than 550 calories, which is hard to believe considering the portions and taste. Yet I purchase, consume, and trust.

I used to own and operate a rice pudding company. I did this for about twelve years from my home. Aside from the annual visits from the Department of Agriculture, who inspected the kitchen for proper food handling equipment and procedures, there was no organization that inspected the rice pudding itself. I personally hired a laboratory to assess the nutritional content for the label, and I trusted that the information they gave me was correct. I trusted them enough that I placed the results of their analysis on my product label. Then, of course, the customers trusted the information on the label when they purchased the product. Truthfully though, I could have put anything in that pudding, and nobody would have had any idea what I was doing. We trust, and we have a lot to lose: our money, our health, and potentially even our lives.

Why then do many people today refuse to trust in or even believe in God? It doesn't cost a thing. There is no risk involved. There is only everything to gain. Some people refuse to believe that which they cannot see, but as I noted above, we do this daily. The same people will trust what they read in history books but refuse to trust the Bible. They will watch the news on television yet scoff at the Good News. They believe that a scientist can determine the age of a fossil dating back billions of years, but simply will not acknowledge the possibility that there is a much, much bigger picture than meets the eye.

Is it a matter of intelligence? Albert Einstein said: "Information is not knowledge." As many of the previous examples proved, the information we are fed does not necessarily make us more knowledgeable, maybe just more gullible.

So how do we obtain real knowledge? Whom do you trust to give you the true information that will make you knowledgeable? St. Augustine said, "Do not go outside, go back into yourself, the heart of the creature lives in the truth."

I challenge you to sit in the silence and listen to the truth that will speak within you. Once you've heard it, you will know and you will trust, and it will be much more real than anything tangible. It will be much more trustworthy than any information you will absorb on this earth.

"I tell you, on the day of judgment
you will have to give an account
for every careless word you utter;
for by your words you will be justified,
and by your words you will be condemned."

Matthew 12:36-37

W.A.I.T. AND LISTEN

I recently met a woman who trains horses. She loves them and talks to them all the time. "Jane" said her horses are wonderful listeners, the best in her life in fact. They instinctively know when she is down, and they comfort her with their gentle, attentive, and loving presence. Jane explained the silent communication so well that I started envisioning the interaction.

Suddenly my brain shifted to "Mr. Ed," and I thought how annoying it would be if the horses started to speak back. Jane didn't need advice or words of any sort. She just needed someone to listen, to hear what she had to say, to sit with her as she walked through her pain or joy, and to simply allow her to express her feelings. What a lesson there for me.

When I think of communication, I automatically think of speaking. How well do I communicate? Pretty darn well, I think. I speak clearly and concisely, and I make sure that the other person understands my words. Communication involves non-verbal gestures as well, however: a simple hug or smile, a wink or nod, a handshake or holding hands, not to mention doing nothing at all but simply listening.

We often get the most comfort from animals who just sit there and listen to us. They seem to know what we're feeling, and somehow, they even seem to walk through the pain with us. They don't respond, sympathize, or judge; they just sit there, giving us the gift of their loving presence. We don't feel frustrated or angry; we feel understood, and that is comfort enough.

My spiritual director once told me to WAIT when I feel the need to respond. It's a wise and handy acronym that reminds me to ask myself: "Why Am I Talking?" I have to be honest, though: I don't use it enough. For some reason, I have the unfounded idea that the other person needs my opinion, not my presence. Even in situations where there is nothing at all to say, I feel I must say something, and that is usually the worst thing I can do. If someone is venting, grieving, or suffering in any way, what on Earth could I possibly say that can help? They just need a loving ear, someone fully present, to hear them and to listen.

I've always said, "Love is an action." I guess I don't think of listening as being an action. Yet a warm and sincere hug is much more powerful than a spoken "I love you." A gentle hand wiping away a tear is much more powerful than a spoken "I'm sorry." A glistening eye, a squeeze of the hand, and a kiss on the cheek all speak volumes and might actually be hampered if followed by spoken words.

In a technological society that is sorely lacking in basic human contact, nothing can be more powerful than a simple touch. We long to be connected in a very basic, human way: to be touched, to be heard, to be loved. Today I am going to remind myself to be quiet and simply WAIT.

> *"In the beginning when God created
> the heavens and the earth,
> the earth was a formless void and darkness
> covered the face of the deep, while a wind
> from God swept over the face of the waters."*
>
> **Genesis 1:1-2**

WHAT MOVES YOU?

Studying astronomy is giving me a whole new perspective on life. Although I've always been aware of and fascinated by our infinite universe, I never really took the time to educate myself about it. Sure, I've seen pictures of our galaxy, and I've learned a bit from those cute little models that the kids made in elementary school. I've seen videos of the first man on the moon, a few pictures of planets, and photos of the Earth from space, but that's about it. Other than that, I pretty much sit here in the middle of inexplicable phenomena, balanced perfectly amidst forces and chemicals, planets, and stars. Yet somehow, I manage to simplify life to that which I can conjure up in my mind or what this tiny little world tells me is true. Crazy.

One thing that really intrigues me is the concept and reality that everything in the universe is in motion. The Earth, the planets, the stars, the chemicals, the forces, all of it — everything out there is in motion. Nothing is static. I get exhausted just thinking about it! My life continues as the physical organs work and move. The stars live on as their chemicals continue to fuse. Gravity is constantly at work; just a constant necessary force. Round and round it all goes, beating, fusing, pulling, pushing, falling, spinning, rotating, revolving – AWESOME!

The interesting thing is that all of the motion has purpose. It's all working to sustain or create new life. The universe isn't just a random set of movements that create chaos. It is beautiful, awesome, and ordered motion, constantly creating new entities, the majority of which we will probably never know.

I believe there's a lesson there for us busy, bustling, and always moving people here on Earth. What is our motion about? Is it ordered? Are we creating something new, beautiful, meaningful, and purposeful? Or are we moving carelessly and creating chaos in our lives and the lives of those around us?

Sometimes we try so hard to create that which will happen naturally if we just let it be. There is plenty occurring without our input, and it's far beyond anything we could ever conjure up on our own. There is a power that is far beyond ours. We can learn a thing or two from our universe which does nothing except be moved by the Mover.

Thomas Aquinas said this is one of the proofs of the existence of God: ". . . things are in motion; anything moved is moved by another; there must be a first mover (a mover that isn't itself moved by another). This is God."

Now *that's* moving. I'm going to try to simply be moved today.

"Whatever your task, put yourselves into it, as done for the Lord and not for your masters."

Colossians 3:23

"I have set before you life and death, blessings and curses. Choose life so that you and your descendants may live."

Deuteronomy 30:19

Fully Alive

It was the perfect summer day. The sky was mostly clear with a few fluffy white clouds slowly floating by. There was a soft, cool breeze. The birds were chirping, and the butterflies were flitting. I could hear the sound of a lawnmower in the distance and the shouts of the kids playing softball at the local high school. Surprisingly, I actually took time to sit lazily in the yard to simply relax and enjoy it all. My neurotic dog was even relaxing under a tree. As I sat there soaking in the sun, I thought to myself: "It's a wonderful day to be alive."

Saint Irenaeus said, "The glory of God is man fully alive." What does it mean to be fully alive? Are there certain basic needs for us to feel fully human?

My dad recently had an operation and was left unable to swallow. Prior to the operation, he was perfectly fine. It was a common procedure with very little risk involved. Today he is home unable to swallow even a drop of water. He has a feeding tube. Is he fully alive?

There is a man from Australia I've seen on YouTube who was born with no arms and legs; what about him? There are people in captivity, people deathly ill, some are blind, deaf, or both. There are people with no family and people who are hungry, illiterate, emotionally unstable, psychologically disturbed, or severely depressed. Are they or do they even have the capacity to be fully alive, fully human?

I believe that we hold deep within us everything we need to be fully alive. We all have different abilities, disabilities, and circumstances, but each of us has something invisible within us that is enough to be fully human. That's not to say that some of us don't need assistance to discover this core and to awaken it. We may need medication, or assistance, or encouragement, but there is no doubt that within us is something supernatural and marvelous. There is something within us that keeps us persevering through the hardest times and can also give us much more than that.

It's not the weather, the food, the visions, or the sounds. It's not our talents or our jobs, our houses or our towns. It's not even our bodies, our age, or our appearance. It's something so deep we can almost overlook it because we're so busy looking around us and outside of us. There's a spirit inside that can survive on its own. It doesn't listen to the loud voices. It doesn't see the extravagance that surrounds us.

It is simple. It is quiet. It is the essence of joy. It is love.

> *"Like good stewards of the manifold grace of God, serve one another with whatever gift each of you has received."*
>
> 1 Peter 4:10

Success Through Service

If you've ever been to a high school basketball game, you've probably heard the "success" cheer. You know, the one that spells it out for you: "S-U-C-C-E-S-S, that's the way you spell success!"

At a basketball game, success obviously means winning. What about in life? What constitutes success? We can chant the cheer all day long and certainly know the spelling, but at the end of the day, were we successful? More importantly, how do *you* define success? I was talking with a friend recently, and she said she felt like a failure. I asked her what would make her successful and how exactly did she define success? She responded: "I don't know."

The dictionary has several definitions of the word "success." Many of them are centered on the attainment of wealth and honors, but the first definition (dictionary.com) defines success as: "the accomplishment of one's goals." That sounds like a reasonable definition, but I've accomplished many preset goals only to end up feeling generally unsuccessful and looking for yet another project to tackle that will make me feel adequate. No matter what I seem to do or accomplish, I haven't found that elusive thing that might contain success.

I hate to constantly blame culture, media, and society, but I think we need to be aware of what surrounds us and what shapes our ideas. It's kind of hard to feel adequate when society tells me that I must be young, have a flawless body, a new car, and a large home. It's not enough anymore to be "just a wife and mother;" a woman has to work, go to school, cook and clean, drive her children to every activity imaginable (the more, the better), and keep her man happy. We've been driven to extremes by the media during holidays as we try to recreate Hallmark commercials and movies that leave us feeling "less than" if we haven't created picture-perfect memories. Celebration parties and weddings have become spectacles and are never good enough anyway.

For all of our efforts, where are we as a society? Are we a bunch of successful, fulfilled families and individuals? Of course not. We're a miserable, medicated mess! So why do we strive for success? What is it that we expect success to give us that we do not possess? I suppose it's a sense of self-worth, a validation that we have purpose and meaning, and that our lives are not pointless. Maybe, if we are successful at work, school, and home (or better yet all three), we can substantiate our existence. I believe it's a modern response to the age-old question: "Why am I here?" Rather than looking inward for the answer, we reach out, groping, flailing, and eventually drowning in our own desperation.

If success is the "attainment of one's goals," let's look at the big picture. At the end of your life when you are in a hospital bed, bidding farewell to loved ones, what successes will you be remembering? Will it be that promotion? That diploma? That huge house or beach home? Will it be that fancy car? The granite countertops? The designer wardrobe? The expensive vacations and beautiful boat? Rather, will you be thinking that you "missed the boat completely?" You had this one opportunity to do "something," but you now realize you weren't successful at all.

Today we might ask ourselves: "What is our life's goal?" Aristotle said: "All men seek one goal: success or happiness. The only way to achieve true success is to express yourself completely in service to society." He's a smart guy, that Aristotle. The only way to true fulfillment is through abandoning our ego and pride and focusing on the betterment of society and others. It's free, simple, and it never goes out of style. In the game of life, our success cheer should be: "S-E-R-V-I-C-E, that's the way we spell success!"

"Be like those who are waiting
for their master
to return from the wedding banquet,
so that they may
open the door for him
as soon as he comes and knocks."

Luke 12:36

Life's Waiting Room

One day, I took my daughter's cat to the vet. While in the waiting area, I observed and talked with some of the others waiting with their pets. There is a simple, but genuine love and pride that fills the room at the veterinarian's office. You don't get any of that pretentious, competitive, defensive, or stand-offish stuff that you get in other waiting rooms. I hate to sound goofy, but it really is that unconditional love that the pets have for their masters and the masters have for their pets. There is affection abounding everywhere. They are mutually and perfectly comfortable in the other's company, and it's so contagious that it spreads to all who enter.

It's like there's an unspoken bond between everyone in the room. We all have pets, and we are taking good care of them. Our pets love us, we love them, and we all love each other. We talk as if the pets are babies (in exaggerated, high-pitched voices, of course!), smile a lot, ask questions, and introduce our pets. We all agree that they are all so beautiful, even the funny-looking pets. It doesn't matter how big or small; how young or old; black, white, tan, or mixed. It's all about love, trust, and protection, and it's all quite simple. There are no mean people here; we're all just one happy, pet-loving family.

Take the pets out of the room, and you'd have a whole different scenario. Suddenly there's no common bond. So what if we're all human? You might be mean, and I might be ignored if I talk to you. I am dressed differently, and your cell phone looks more expensive than mine. What kind of car did you drive here in? Oh, you're like *that*. There's no trust, no love, and it's all about protecting ourselves from being hurt.

I wish my furry friend was by my side. He'd show you how great I am, and I'd show you how great he is. Together we feel safe, and we just want to share our love with everyone around us.

Alone, I feel too vulnerable, so I'd rather just sit quietly and stare at my phone until the nurse comes and rescues me from the discomfort of sitting amidst strangers who might be staring and judging me.

That love that we get from our pets can be carried with us everywhere we go, and we don't have to own a pet or a pet carrier to have it with us. It takes work, risk, and especially prayer, because (someone once told me) it isn't a coincidence that the word God is dog spelled backwards.
Okay, I know that's a stretch, but just imagine that God was by our side instead of our furry friends. Imagine the love, peace, joy, and sense of security in *that* waiting room.

That's exactly where we are right now: in *that* waiting room with our God by our side.

> *"Trust in the Lord with all your heart, and do not rely on your own insight. In all your ways acknowledge him, and he will make straight your paths."*
>
> **Proverbs 3:5-6**

Trust Me

I cannot think of too many words as potent as the word "trust." It's not a word that we throw around lightly, unless perhaps we are being sarcastic, such as, "I trust that you will be home by midnight."

Let's try something. Complete this sentence: "Of all the people on Earth, I trust _____."

My guess is that many of us have a very short list. If you've picked up a newspaper or watched the news in any given twenty-four-hour period, you've certainly questioned your ability to trust. We're constantly inundated with stories of teachers, students, doctors, dentists, nurses, politicians, clergy, husbands, wives, children, and every other form of human being who have shocked friends and relatives with some bizarre reality (often lethal) that nobody ever would have suspected. If that seems distant and doesn't impact you, then surely you've experienced some less troubling form of mistrust at home. I'm not sure what's worse, the horrific shocks we hear on television, or the small stings we withstand all too often on the home front.

There's no way around it: trust is risky business. There is always the chance that we are going to be hurt, and history, the news, and our personal experiences prove that we probably will be. So, what are our options here? We can isolate ourselves and have no human interaction, but that's rather cowardly. We can choose to be bitter, jaded, resentful, and angry, but that's ineffective. Finally, we can realize that we have choices and do not have to be completely vulnerable. We can choose to be careful about exactly what we decide to share, take, or give away in our relationships. We can choose to say yes, no, I'm not sure, or I'm not ready. We can ask questions and communicate frequently on a level that helps us to feel safe and understood. We can proceed slowly and in a manner that makes us feel secure. We can pace ourselves and act intentionally. Once we realize that we have choices and are not victims, we will have less fear.

In relationships, we must realize that everything begins within ourselves. We have everything we need inside of us to keep us safe in many common situations. The sad thing is that we don't even trust ourselves. We shut down our inner voice or never even take the time to listen to it. We look outward to others for answers, strength, and love that we first must discover on our own from within. Only then will we feel totally free to take that leap of faith and reach out to trust another.

When I am centered and spiritually strong and healthy, it is much easier for me to risk being vulnerable with another person because I am not stumbling blindly in the dark groping for fulfillment. Rather, I am taking an intentional, practiced, exhilarating leap of faith into the refreshing pool of life. If occasionally I belly flop, I'll be certain to be more careful next time. I probably acted too quickly and without focus. It's simply a lesson, a reminder, and another chance for me to get it right next time. It's all worth it. Trust me.

(painting by my daughter Jenna)

*"But speaking the truth in love,
we must grow up in every way
into him who is the head, into Christ."*

Ephesians 4:15

The Reality of Relationships

My mom calls me every year to wish me a happy anniversary. At the time of this writing, my husband and I are celebrating 31 years of marriage together. I still feel like the nineteen-year-old girl I was when we met, yet I've changed so much largely because of my husband. He brings out the best in me, he loves the worst in me, and he has taught me what love is.

Sadly, many people cannot say that about their spouses, friends, or family members. So often people settle for mediocrity in relationships mainly because fear prevents them from going deeper. I have found that relationships must constantly be attended to, they must be shaped and formed into something beautiful. It's kind of like sculpting. You make an adjustment here or there, step back, and have a look at it. The next day you have another look, and something seems a little bit off, so you fix that. Maybe that adjustment moved something else out of whack, so you try again. It doesn't end, it's never quite finished, but it's not a job; it's a hobby. It's a special gift that's been given to you, and you enjoy it and the work it requires. It's all a part of the gift.

I didn't go into this relationship with my husband knowing anything at all about relationships. We fought like crazy when we were dating! Even the early years of our marriage were spent arguing. No, that's way too gentle of a word. We fought, we screamed, slammed doors, kicked walls, threw things, etc. We fought to be heard and understood.

The Bible says: ". . . a man will leave his father and mother and be united to his wife, and the two will become one flesh" (Genesis 2:24). That sounds so sweet and simple. Well, we struggled a lot for our individual identity as we were being transformed from two into one. We fought our way into creating a new identity as one.

Think about what a traumatic process that has to be: two becoming one flesh. It's downright volatile, and that's the way it was.

Once we survived the "sculpting" that transformed us from two to one, the work wasn't finished. That new creation had to be safeguarded, cared for, and it required routine maintenance. It still does.

A relationship defined is simply "a connection, association, or involvement," but I beg to differ that it is much, much more than that. That definition sounds to me like a relationship between some non-living things. If you think about it, any person, place, or thing that has a connection, association, or involvement with another is going to somehow affect the other person, place, or thing. Two blocks placed side by side on a table might cast a shadow on the table or reflect color onto the other block. When you place two things together, or side by side, there is going to be some sort of reaction, positive or negative. Add in all the complexities of human beings, and you've got yourself quite an array of reactions.

We all experience that on a daily basis. We react to the people around us — the people we are in relationship with — constantly, positively or negatively.

So what makes our relationship work? Much of it has to do with trust I think, and there can be no trust without truthful, shameless, candid, and continual *communication*. To be in a relationship, you have to *relate*. That's a verb meaning "to tell." Heart has to speak to heart, and there can be nothing blocking that connection, sharing, and telling. Heart speaking to heart doesn't mean singing sweet love songs to each other. It is often painful and frightening. We have to share everything, the good and the bad, to be able to understand and manage things. There are many people who live with or are in relationships with people they don't really know. There is a desire to share, to communicate, to love, but there is also a fear of being hurt, shamed, or shunned. Yet they continue to interact, to be in relationship, and therefore to react in ways that are unproductive and even harmful. It's unhealthy, it's heartbreaking, and it continues because of fear of rejection or confrontation.

Gandhi said: "Whenever you have truth it must be given with love, or the message and the messenger will be rejected." The truth must be shared and received with love. It's often painful, volatile, and scary, but it's the only way to a real relationship. We are all in relationship anyway — we are all connecting, associating, or involved in some way (family, friends, co-workers, neighbors). We've got one life and the relationships in it are important.

I encourage you to speak your truth, to listen to others' truths, and to speak and listen with love to avoid the fear of rejection. Someone has to be the catalyst; why not you? Take someone special in your life by the hand and show them the way to a beautiful, flourishing, healthy, whole, *real* relationship. Tell them you have to relate to be in relationship. Don't settle for anything less.

> "O give thanks to the Lord,
> for he is good,
> for his steadfast
> love endures forever."

Psalm 136:1

TAPPED OUT?

During an extreme heat wave one year, I awoke to a strange sound coming from the bathroom at 2:30 am. I sat on the tub, shut the door, and listened intently. It was a loud, unidentifiable noise that stopped when I tightened the faucet. When I turned the faucet back on, a burst of air came out. I would have thought the well ran dry, but we have city water, so I figured that was unlikely.

I woke my husband, who stumbled out of bed to investigate. Nothing but air was flowing through all of the water pipes and out of each of the faucets. The inconveniences were immediately apparent as the toilets would not flush, and my dog suddenly became insatiably thirsty. We called the water company's emergency number, and they said they would send someone out. They must have worked through the night, because before noon the next day, the water was back on. During those less than twelve hours, however, we got a glimpse of what life is like without running water. It is a blessing that we simply do not appreciate. It is a blessing that much of the world still does not possess.

Back in 1992, the year my youngest daughter was born, our family experienced another water inconvenience. A local gas station's old tanks leaked gasoline into the town's water supply, and a chemical (now a known carcinogen) was present in the drinking water. The town's response was to direct all the inhabitants across town to fill at a small outdoor pump with jugs. We were told that we could use the water to shower and clean as long as we did so in well-ventilated areas, because inhaling the chemicals was harmful. That sounded absolutely absurd to me, so I ended up lugging something like 20 gallons of water daily to use for cooking, showering, drinking, and the rest. Friends and relatives marveled at my diligence and valor. It's kind of funny thinking about it now. I "lugged" the one-gallon water jugs from the pump about 6 feet to my vehicle and vice versa at the house. It wasn't like I walked miles in the sweltering heat with no shoes and a 20-gallon jug on my head!

There are days when gratitude seems difficult. I'd rather wallow in my own self-pity than to take an honest look at the blessings in my life. Running water has become something that I expect, something I've always had so I presume I always will. What a terribly selfish and small attitude! The Internet provides opportunities for me to expand my mind and horizon to get a glimpse of the struggles the rest of the world endures.

Today I will remember to appreciate the simple blessings in life and to not overlook those things that have somehow become expectations. I will expand my little world to include others on the planet who are less fortunate. I will do my part to reach out in any way that I can to improve the life of another.

"O give thanks to the Lord, for he is good;
for his steadfast love endures forever."

Psalm 107:1

*"The Lord protects the simple;
when I was brought low,
he saved me."*

Psalm 116:6

Training for Simplicity

Once, when my husband and I went to Florida to visit family, we decided to treat ourselves to a roomette on an Amtrak train. For those of you who haven't experienced this, it's a roughly 3' x 6' space that includes two chairs opposite each other that recline into one bed, a bunk that pulls down above the lower bed, an open toilet that is practically one with the chair, a funky fold-away sink, and a small table that folds open between the two chairs. Nothing fancy, but we are simple people, we thought.

We were very excited when we first entered the room at around noon and neatly placed our belongings in the small cubby opposite the upper bunk. What a fun way to travel! We had our own little sanctuary for 24 hours where no one could reach us, and we were grateful for everything, including the free water, coffee, and juice. We quickly opened the folding table; placed our laptop, iPad, and books on it; and settled in for a day of relaxation and productivity in our small, cozy space.

So the day continued as we marveled at our good fortune of being able to have peace and quiet in our own intimate room. I finally finished a book I started reading months ago and began another. We both made some important phone calls, settled some insurance matters, and other miscellaneous tasks in between trips to the dining car for meals. The small inconvenience of the open toilet began to get on our nerves as I had to send Mark out of the room at least five times throughout the day. (We're married over thirty years, but there are still things that we both consider private. Using the toilet is one of them.)

After dinner, we returned to the roomette excited to transform the place into our sleeping quarters. Like children, we jumped into bed and watched a video while snuggled against each other. So romantic, we thought. We're such simple people. Another couple would probably not appreciate this. After the movie, Mark gallantly climbed to the top bunk to settle in for a good night's sleep, and I remained below with a smile on my face as I drifted off to sleep somewhere in the Carolinas, I think.

It wasn't long before the sound of the train's incessantly blaring horn awoke me, and I figured I might as well use the toilet while I was awake. To heck with the modesty, I told Mark to close his ears and eyes and deal with it…at least five times throughout the night! AT LEAST FIVE TIMES throughout the night this happened. Needless to say, I didn't get much sleep, and neither did Mark, as I had to keep waking him to tell him to close his eyes!

Around 4:00 a.m., after listening to the horn all night, someone's alarm clock went off and continued for about an hour. By now, my husband was awake, and the two of us were complaining about the idiot in the next room who just wouldn't get up to shut off the alarm. I started mumbling obscenities after about a half hour, then Mark chimed in with obnoxious sounds that kind of sounded like a muffled, "Shut the alarm!" Before you know it, I was threatening to get a weapon. What the heck was wrong with the person, and why wasn't the attendant doing anything?

After about an hour of this, Mark quietly and casually said, "I think that's *my* alarm!!" He jumped up and fumbled through the cubby to pull out the suitcase that contained his cell phone and silenced his alarm. After the thirty-minute laughing fit that followed, we were finally able to fall asleep for a few hours. The next morning, we upgraded to a "real" room for the return trip. So much for simplicity that time, but we'll keep trying.

"The people who sat in darkness
have seen a great light,
and for those who sat in the region
and shadow of death
light has dawned."

Matthew 4:16

Out of the Darkness

Sometimes I wake up in the middle of the night, and I feel my way to the bathroom. It's sort of a stressful few minutes as I reach around to feel the walls and walk slowly so I don't stub my toe on anything. I'm a bit apprehensive, but I know at the end of this rather uncomfortable trek, I will flip a switch, and there will be light. Once the light appears, instantly I feel a relief, peace flowing through me. I can see clearly, and the fear is gone.

Nobody chooses to physically stay in darkness. We all innately seek light. During the winter months, we count the hours to the spring and summer when the days will be longer and brighter. Sunny days generally bring us more energy and zest, and dark, gloomy days often bring us down both emotionally and physically. In a dark room, our eyes automatically seek out any small speck of light. Our pupils grow larger and larger to help us to see. When we find light, we focus on it, and that is where we find comfort. When we were kids playing hide and seek and we had to count to ten with our eyes closed, it took all we had to wait before we would joyfully open our eyes to see exactly what was around us. Relief! Now we could get down to the business of finding our friends.

While we automatically seek light physically, we sometimes choose to stay in the dark emotionally and spiritually. Perhaps the light in some cases seems more frightening than the dark. Sometimes when we flip the switch and look in the mirror, the reflection is not as pretty as we'd imagined. Better to shut the light and stay in the dark where our illusions can be whatever we want them to be. The problem is that we cannot see clearly in the dark, and except for mold or fungi, not much can grow there. We can only hope to, at best, remain stagnant. To grow, we must bring ourselves slowly into the light, squinting if necessary, so as not to blind ourselves, but advancing all the same.

I heard someone say recently that remaining "in the dark" can be either a womb or a tomb. In the womb, one is comforted, nurtured, and nourished. It is a safe and happy place where the fetus can hear sounds, feel things, move, and even smile. It is alive and growing, and it has a vital connection to its life source. Conversely, a tomb offers none of those things. A tomb is filled with death. Nothing is brought to it except a dead body, and nothing is hoped to ever come from it. It has no hope for growth. It is lifeless. Both are dark spaces, but each is drastically different.

A good question to ask ourselves might be: "Am I choosing to remain in the dark?" Temporarily, the space might be a womb of sorts. (It's important to remember that a womb's purpose is to protect, nurture, and ultimately produce new life. It is not a permanent dwelling place.) Conversely, have we created a tomb for ourselves? Have we buried ourselves so deeply that we cannot see the light or bring forth new life?

The good news is that the tomb you may be in is not physical, and you can therefore come out of it. You may have to squint, and you will likely need a few hands to help you, but you can, in fact, come out of the tomb. The light will kill the mold and fungi, and it will burn away anything that is stagnant. You will be refreshed and renewed, but you must first remove the blindfold and follow any hint of a pure light source. If finding a light switch in the middle of the night provides relief and erases fear, imagine the joy you will experience once you have come out of the darkness of the tomb and into the "marvelous light" (1 Peter 2:9).

"Every generous act of giving, with every perfect gift, is from above, coming down from the Father of lights, with whom there is no variation or shadow due to change."

James 1:17

A Present or a Privilege?

I was listening to a comedian one morning, and he was discussing the fact that he is an atheist. Though most of his comments were simple and funny, his final comment was quite assertive and caused me to think for a moment. He said, "My take is this: If I get up to heaven, and there is a God, and he says: 'you were wrong, so how did you live your life?'" The comedian replied: "I tried to help people. I gave to charity. I didn't know if you were real, and there was no evidence." God replied: "Well, you didn't worship me every day." The comedian responded: "Fine! Send me wherever is as far away from you as possible, because you're a sociopath." Nervy, don't you think?

I'd had a similar comment from a family member that summer. We were conversing about the fact that he only attends church periodically. I explained that one of God's commandments is to keep the Sabbath holy, and as my cousin is also Catholic, that means attending church every Sunday. He said something like, "If God is not going to let me into Heaven because I don't go to Church regularly, then that's a god I don't want to be with." Wow.

We've certainly come to a point in society where we feel a sense of entitlement. These remarks seem to imply that we're here doing what *we believe* is best for us, for God, and for the world, and if God doesn't think so...well, who needs Him? What does He know? We can just stamp our self-righteous, self-sustaining feet, throw our little human tantrums, and disown this invisible God because He's too ungrateful and doesn't appreciate how good we are!

Have we forgotten, or perhaps never stopped to consider, that our very being is a gift? We don't *deserve* to be here. We don't *have* to be here. Do any of us really have a clue as to *how* to be here without some serious divine guidance? Our life should be spent in obedience, worship, prayer, and thanksgiving because we are so eternally grateful to the One who has given everything to us.

I don't know about you, but when someone gives me a gift, I usually send a thank you note. The gift makes me feel special, loved, and so grateful for the person who gave it to me. My response is an act of love in return for the love shown to me. So what's my response when I wake up to the gift of life in the morning? Thank you! What's my response when I feel the brisk fall breeze and see the beautiful changing leaves? Glory to God! What's my response when I feel my heartbeat? Awesome! The more grateful I become, the more visible the gifts become, and the more I am inclined to worship, love, pray, and adore.

Maybe instead of focusing on the rules, we should see our need for guidance. The commandments are there *for us*. They are a blessing, not a curse. Instead of expecting more from God, perhaps we should start by thanking Him for what He has already given us. Instead of thinking that we could possibly even begin to know the answers, let's start listening and pondering those things that just might contain more wisdom than we could ever conceive in our little minds. I guarantee you that when you accept, embrace, and act according to God's desires, YOU will be the one to receive, not God. He's a little smarter than you think.

*"The thief comes only
to steal and kill and destroy.
I came that they may have life,
and have it abundantly."*

John 10:10

"You shall love the Lord your God
with all your heart,
and with all your soul,
and with all your strength,
and with all your mind;
and your neighbor as yourself."

Luke 10:27

I Resolve...
Problem Solved

Sometimes life seems so long. Despite the frequent claims of the apocalypse, a new day dawns without fail, and here I am to face it. I awoke one morning from a miserable dream and made my way downstairs for a cup of coffee. The pain in my lower back reminded me that I needed to stretch. The cat was leading the way to his food bowl, and the dog couldn't wait another second to go outside. There was laundry on the floor and dishes in the sink. Scraps of last night's movie snacks were still on the coffee table. Here we go. Another day.

My thoughts turned to the circumstances in my life, others' lives, and the world as I began to wash the dishes and gaze out the window. Nothing seemed especially good right now. My subconscious was on a roll, and everywhere it turned there was conflict, pain, and drama. I started imagining ways that I can fix the situations, and a few times I was certain a particular plan would work. However, my mind was not convinced, so it kept on spinning until I was feeling confused and uncertain as to what I am to do. Finally, my eyes began to focus on my immediate surroundings, and they fell upon a small rock on the ledge of the window. It was a rock that my youngest daughter painted in elementary school a million years ago. It simply says: "God." I smiled as I realized that my focus had been on every problem I could think of, but I had not for one moment focused on the solution.

Imagine the possibilities if I spend all of my waking hours focusing always on God. I keep proving to myself time and time again that my ways do not work. The changes I seek do not come from anywhere other than God. Believe me, I've tried. That morning, I was graced with the realization that all of these things I am obsessing on are becoming my God. St. Paul's letter to the Colossians 3:2 reads: "Set your mind on the things above, not on the things that are on earth."

If you don't believe them, maybe you'll believe Einstein. He is quoted as having said, "When the solution is simple, God is answering." There it is: the solution, pure and simple. Today I will focus on the solution, not the problem.

> "O give thanks to the Lord, call on his name, make known his deeds among the peoples."
>
> **Psalm 105:1**

THANKS AND GIVING

I'd like to sit here and write a beautiful Thanksgiving reflection, but truly Thanksgiving through New Year's Day is my least favorite time of year. I probably just need some serious psychotherapy, but if one more person asks me what I'm doing for Thanksgiving, or tells me how many people they are entertaining, or how big their turkey is . . . I'm going to lose it! I'm sure there was a time, maybe 200 years ago, when Thanksgiving really was an American holiday that celebrated our history. That's long gone. Now it's a competition, yet another excuse for shopping and spending, and the kickoff to the season of materialism (all in the name of reputable traditions of course) to save us from the shame of the reality.

Holidays nowadays are fraught with expectations, and I've learned that expectations are premeditated resentments. I don't wait for the after-effect; I get resentful during the expectation phase. What would happen if we set our expectations higher than those decided for us by television commercials? What would happen if the entire country sacrificed the turkey dinners, parties, trees, lights, cookies, pies, and gifts, or even just a fraction of them, and instead helped the people in the Philippines or any of the other countless people who would be happy to simply receive a word of encouragement and hope? Better yet, what if we didn't need a season to remind us to do these things, but rather did them every single day of our lives?

I realize these traditions are all in the name of something good, but the road to hell is paved with good intentions. Instead of a cookie swap party this year, let's have everyone bring the money for the ingredients and send it to the Red Cross. We could play Christmas music and write cards to soldiers. How about we invite those neighbors we never speak to: the outcast, the elderly, or the lonely? Why do we have to cram all of this in from November to January? How would our lives and world change if this was simply part of our everyday life?

St. Paul reminds us in his first letter to the Thessalonians: "We urge you, brothers, admonish the idle, cheer the fainthearted, support the weak, be patient with all. See that no one returns evil for evil; rather; always seek what is good for each other and for all. Rejoice always. Pray without ceasing. In all circumstances give thanks, for this is the will of God for you in Christ Jesus." That was written a heck of a long time before the American Thanksgiving holiday. To think, there was no mention of a turkey!

*"Give, and it will be given to you.
A good measure, pressed down,
shaken together, running over,
will be put into your lap;
for the measure you give
will be the measure you get back."*

Luke 6:38

"No one who practices deceit
shall remain in my house;
no one who utters lies
shall continue in my presence."

Psalm 101:7

Are You For Real??!!

Would someone please explain to me why everyone is so outraged and shocked over the fact that Lance Armstrong used drugs and that he lied about it? Since when are we a culture of truth and purity, infuriated because a personality is not whom they claimed to be? This deceit has been going on forever. Maybe we're finally just not going to take it anymore. I somehow doubt that, though.

Don't get me wrong – I hate it – but it doesn't surprise me one bit. It's gotten to the point where I don't know what the heck is real anymore, and that's an ugly place to be. Why bother establishing friendships? Who can we trust to turn to for guidance? Do we really know our own families? What are the real intentions of the politicians? Why all the secrets? Why are we afraid, like the old song, "to be real?"

Nobody likes being lied to, and Lance pretended to be something he wasn't. Let's face it, though – we probably could have figured out that something wasn't right. In my experience, there are clues or maybe even just instincts that lead us to suspect something is amiss, but we look away and join right in with the pretending. Then we get hurt and feel duped when we are partly to blame ourselves. It's all a ridiculous game, and it's no fun. We need to stop playing, trust our guts, and stop putting faith, expectations, and zeal in other people.

Thomas Aquinas said: "As a matter of honor, one man owes it to another to manifest the truth." You see, it begins with you and me. If I want to hear less lies, all I can do is be truthful. If I want to see more success, I can work on flourishing. If I want the world to change, I can move myself to initiate change. If we make the mistake of putting another person up on a pedestal (like Lance), we can at least put a hand out to help him up when he falls, because he couldn't have put himself up there without our help.

So what is it that we can know for certain? What on Earth is real and true? This isn't something tangible that you can go purchase at the local mall. This isn't something you can demand from another person or entity. It's something supernatural that requires time, attention, and work, and that work begins within each and every one of us.

What is real? Well, let's start with you and me. If I take off my mask and make myself vulnerable, will you do the same? Will you accept me with all my imperfections and reveal your flaws and fears to me? Will we support each other in truth and love? That's a start, and that's the best we can do.

"You desire truth in the inward being; therefore teach me wisdom in my secret heart."

Psalm 51:6

"Listen, I will tell you a mystery!
We will not all die,
but we will all be changed,
in a moment,
in the twinkling of an eye,
at the last trumpet.
For the trumpet will sound,
and the dead will be raised imperishable,
and we will be changed."

1 Corinthians 15:51-52

Twinkle, Twinkle Little Star

I love to contemplate the universe. Sometimes it's easy, and it really helps to put my life in the proper perspective. It keeps me humble and open-minded, because in the grand scheme of things, my tiny brain is really a speck of dust. Other times I am so consumed in myself and my small world, that I actually forget the big picture. During those times I become anxious, fearful, indignant, selfish, and egotistical. I get caught up in doing, controlling, and fixing, and I don't set aside the time to pray and reflect. I need to remember what it's all about. Genesis 3:19 reminds me: "By the sweat of your face you shall eat bread until you return to the ground, for out of it you were taken; *you are dust, and to dust you shall return.*"

When I finally took a moment for reflection, I got to thinking about the universe expansion theory (yeah, I know that's not normal!). It just fascinates me that the Earth is but a crumb amidst an infinite and expanding universe. I considered the formation of new stars, and I thought: Imagine if each new star being formed is a soul that has been lifted up and is in a state of transition. It's like a purgatory of sorts as the various changes take place until a new star emerges and shines brightly in all its splendor. Envision the entire expanding universe as an immeasurable heaven, surrounding us with light, promise, and security.

I'm no scientist, but I know a little about the formation of stars, and that formation begins "within clouds of *dust*." There is a powerful force involved, including pressure and fusion. It's a magnificent process and a continual one, a process of dust, motion, force, collapse, and rebirth. It is absolutely awesome. St. Paul tells us: "There are both heavenly bodies and earthly bodies, but the glory of the heavenly is one thing, and that of the earthly is another. There is one glory of the sun, and another glory of the moon, and another glory of the stars; indeed, star differs from star in glory" (1 Corinthians 15:40-41). Yes they do, as do souls.

It's an exciting world and universe, an astonishing life surrounded by infinite mysteries. All of it involves *dust*, force, motion, light, darkness, birth, death, and rebirth. It's happening all around us, and we take it for granted. We are shrouded in mystery yet given many promises. Look up and around! Pray and believe, and let your light shine here on Earth.

*"When I look at your heavens,
the work of your fingers,
the moon and the stars
that you have established;
what are human beings
that you are mindful of them,
mortals that you care for them?"*

Psalm 8:3-4

"Guard what has been entrusted to you. Avoid the profane chatter and contradictions of what is falsely called knowledge."

1 Timothy 6:20

We Are But Dust

Have you ever heard of that show *Cosmos* on Fox? Fortunately for my mental state, I do not have cable television (just Roku on which I mainly watch Netflix), but out of curiosity I started watching episode one online. If you've read my blog in the past, you know I have a real interest in astronomy. Unlike scientists though, my interest and limited exploration/knowledge of it doesn't inflate my ego — it deflates it. The scope and grandeur of the universe leaves me feeling simple and small.

The first thing I noticed about *Cosmos* was that it seemed to want to show just how smart we humans are. Look what we've figured out! We've got this god-like thing called science that can tell us everything we need to know when we test, experiment, and observe. Look how far we've come and how far we're going in the future! Sorry, guys, but it didn't work for me.

I admit that I didn't watch the entire episode. I turned it off after a very spectacular and insightful visual. The camera somehow took viewers through myriads of solar systems — each one looking like specks of nothingness in the black abyss. At one point, the camera stopped for a moment to point out which dot was our solar system — not even the earth — the entire solar system. There it was, a grain of sand called the Milky Way. Unbelievable. That was enough for me because, call me cynical, I don't believe that anyone on that grain knows a whole heck of a lot about anything. Believe it or not,

Oh Great and Powerful Science, there is a power much greater than you.

What I found perhaps even more fascinating was that on this tiniest of dots in the universe — we live in the incomprehensible vastness of it all with minds that are so intricately programmed so as to seek upward and outward. Why? How? Our minds really are pretty powerful when you look at the big picture (not as powerful as science would like us to think, but still pretty darn good!). It's amazing! Not only are we here on this crumb with bodies that are designed greater than any fine-tuned machine made by man, but we have these computers in our heads that came out long before Windows 95! Additionally, we have spiritual beings (currently undetected by infrared or any other scientific gadget) that long for something more than any person, place, or thing on our particle of dust can give us. Yet *Cosmos* wants me to believe that we've got it all covered because we see that we are but dust in the midst of more dust. What am I missing?

What keeps coming to my mind since watching the show is the Dr. Seuss book "Horton Hears a Who." Horton the elephant hears a cry from a speck of dust on a clover, which turns out to be home to a whole community of people. Horton does his best to protect the speck because his neighbors don't believe that anything lives on it. They become quite arrogant and nasty, and they try to destroy the dust and Horton in the process. Horton protects the dust until he can finally prove the existence of the Whos in Whoville who live on the dust. Science would've killed the darn thing by pulling it apart and placing it under a microscope. Finally, they all heard the voices of the people, and they believed.

There is a God — currently invisible to the naked eye. Some of us carry Him around (like Horton) and try to protect Him from an arrogant world of non-believers who refuse to trust what they cannot observe, what they cannot test on our speck of dust. They do their best to hush up the people who hear Him and to try to destroy anything that we point to as proof because they themselves cannot hear. Horton persisted, and so must we, because in the grand scheme of things, we are but dust carried on a clover by God, who is protecting us despite the arrogance.

*"Do you wish to rise?
Begin by descending.
You plan a tower that
will pierce the clouds?
Lay first the foundation of humility."*

Saint Augustine

Secular Spirituality

I took a workshop course several weeks ago on spirituality. Before the instructor began his agenda, he went around the room asking each student four questions:

1. What was your spiritual upbringing?
2. What is your spirituality now?
3. What is your view of humanity, mankind, human nature, etc.?
4. What do you want from this time together?

No two answers were the same: "I'm an atheist...I'm a secular humanist...I don't believe in your religion...I am finally free of the guilt imposed on me by religion...I believe in the universe... I'm a Buddhist, etc." Arguments ensued from the get-go as degrading comments were carelessly dropped and know-it-all attitudes about the unknown were prevalent. There was a strong tension that never let up, under which I'm certain was a subliminal fear, because at the core of these questions lies each person's foundation. The instructor might just as well have asked: "What are you standing on?"

Spirituality is at the very heart of our being. It has as many definitions as types. One definition is "the lived experience of faith." It has also been described as "the inner quality or nature of a person." Based on the responses in our class that weekend, you would think we all came from different planets with different natures. No one could seem to agree, not even to disagree, and few could be silent and humble. If spirituality is the inner quality or nature of a person, I would like to think that at least one common denominator would be love. From there, we could begin to see our connectedness, and we could begin to converse as the loving, spiritual beings we claim to be.

Beyond all the chaos and meanness, what really saddened me was the lack of awe and respect for the mystery that enshrouds all aspects of life, death, and spirit. Instead, there is a blatant pride and confidence in self and science, and the results of that are being felt everywhere as they were in our small classroom: tension, anxiety, fear, and anger. Sure, we've got that kind of spirituality down pretty good. It's a spirituality of the mind, not the heart. It's a spirituality that believes that all in the heavens and on Earth can be explained only by man and science. I say it's way too simple.

It is said, "prayer is the ascent of the mind towards God." That requires a level of humility -- admitting that there are things that we do not and cannot know. With that simple admission, infinite possibilities open. It's exciting, inspiring, life giving, and hope-filled. My experience tells me that we receive much more by humbling ourselves than by limiting our minds to our own small thoughts. It's okay to say, "I don't know." It's a sign of courage to fall down and cry out. It's a grace to look up in wonder, reverence, and awe. It all begins with a heart full of love and a mind that ascends far beyond itself and the currently known theories of our world.

When my spirit sings, it's not about human theories. My spirit soars way beyond that, and it desires ever more.

"When pride comes,
then comes disgrace,
but wisdom is with the humble."

Proverbs 11:2

"If we confess our sins,
he who is faithful and
just will forgive us our sins
and cleanse us from all unrighteousness."

1 John 1:9

The Window to Your Soul

Lady Bird Johnson is quoted as having said, "Art is the window to man's soul. Without it, he would never be able to see beyond his immediate world; nor could the world see the man within." Obviously, she said that long before postmodernism. Still, the quote gets me thinking about souls, windows, and the ability or inability to see clearly through to one's soul.

Let's imagine our bodies as windows to our souls. What type of glass is your window made of? There are many types of glass, all having various thicknesses and strengths. Some are insulated and contain two or three pieces of glass. Tempered glass is much stronger and safer than others when shattered. Laminated glass is coated to reflect the sunlight (perhaps with a mirrored coating). Float glass is thin, flat, very smooth, and consistent, while annealed glass is a little stronger than float glass, but will break into large, sharp pieces if shattered. There's also wire glass, which is safer if exposed to high heat.

Besides all the various types of glass, you might decide to choose a pattern or texture for your soul's glass window. On a typical window, this feature might be added for privacy or style. On our souls' windows, accessories might be included as a camouflage. Who can blame someone for piling on the embellishments? After all, it's not easy to walk through this world with a thin, clear, easily shattered window for a protective shell! The trimmings are free, right? They're not really free, however, as everything has its price. In this case, the price could be quite high — isolation, weak relationships (with others and with God), lack of self-knowledge, etc. The beauty that lies within each and every one of us cannot be truly appreciated and shared if it is hidden beneath a thick, insulated, tinted, mirrored, textured, or even just a plain old dirty window.

Perhaps it's time to replace our window, or maybe we just need to clean it up a bit. If you have an old window around your house somewhere, or if you see one along the side of the road in your travels, pull it out and set it inside in a place where you'll see it daily. Get yourself a pack of washable markers and write or draw on your window everything that is creating a barrier to your soul. You might write or draw things like guilt, shame, loneliness, anger, fatigue, doubt, gossip, fear, idolatry, relationship issues, selfishness, and greed. I'm sure we can all come up with a list that will more than fill our windows. Make it a fun project — colorful and fancy — perhaps similar to the way we all work so hard at creating that reality in our daily lives.

Then each day (or week or month), try to erase something from the window. Just try to eliminate or resolve one thing that is keeping you from the clarity that you could have and that you deserve. Of course, there will be days when you will have to add back in something that you previously erased, or there will be new things that have to be added in place of old ones that have been cleaned. That's okay! Keep at it — don't give up! Enjoy the process, and don't forget to marvel at the glimmers of sunshine that are sure to make their way through the glass no matter how messy it may get.

> **GOD IS LOVE**
> *"Beloved, let us love one another, because love is from God; everyone who loves is born of God and knows God."*
>
> 1 John 4:7

ALL YOU NEED IS LOVE

A wise woman shared a simple thought with me recently. It was a quote from a *Salada* tea bag from many years ago that read, "What we see depends mainly on what we look for." We have the power within us to see things from various perspectives. It's actually a bit frightening to me! How do we know if what we are seeing is true or if it is simply what we (or others) want us to see?

In some situations, ignorance is bliss and not too destructive, but in other circumstances, we must strive to see the truth. That takes work! It's not easy amidst the chaos of our modern society where millions of messages bombarded us on any given day. It's no wonder anxiety is so prevalent. We are simply not meant to process this amount of information.

Additionally, now that everyone and his/her mother (including me!) has a means to voice his or her opinion, whom do we trust as the true authority? I personally have swayed back and forth on some issues. In some instances, ignorance was bliss, and I was better off not knowing the latest teachings on a given subject. In other circumstances, it was absolutely essential that I know more and not rely on my basic education of the subject. In those cases, I was surprised at how my thoughts shifted with the new knowledge. In all matters, I still consider that anything I think I know is simply what has been taught to me by someone else — and what do they really know?

I have finally and happily come to a beautiful and peaceful place. All I need to know is what I know for certain at the depths of my being. If all of my thoughts and actions flow forth from love, all will be as true as it can possibly be. To give love, I must receive the grace from the One who is love — God.

So, as St. Augustine said: "Love God and do as you please." Once we put God first and focus on loving Him, we will receive everything we need to know, love, and live, so much more than we could ever receive from any source of information here on this earth. As always, St. Paul speaks so eloquently on this:

"If I speak in the tongues of mortals and of angels, but do not have love, I am a noisy gong or a clanging cymbal. And if I have prophetic powers, and understand all mysteries and all knowledge, and if I have all faith, so as to remove mountains, but do not have love, I am nothing. If I give away all my possessions, and if I hand over my body so that I may boast, but do not have love, I gain nothing" (1 Corinthians 13:1-3).

So then if "what we see depends mainly on what we look for," and we are looking for the One who is love, we will see as clearly as we can at this moment and place in time. Again, St. Paul tells us: "For now we see in a mirror, dimly, but then we will see face to face. Now I know only in part; then I will know fully, even as I have been fully known. And now faith, hope, and love abide, these three; and the greatest of these is love" (1 Corinthians 13:12-13).

Today and every day, let's turn off all the noise and look inward and upward to the One who is love for all of the answers we need.

"In the beginning when God created the heavens and the earth."

Genesis 1:1

What's Your Story?

I'd been working on writing and illustrating a children's book for some time now but attempting to edit it was slow going. As I procrastinated editing, I thought about stories in general. I'm sure you've heard it said that "everyone has a story," but I don't think we consider the concept of story itself. A story has elements such as a plot, setting, characters, and a theme. Sometimes I'd like to know who the heck is writing my story, because frankly, there are times when I think I would have written it quite differently!

So what role *do* I have in writing my story? Am I a co-author or merely a character? It seems apparent to me that I am a co-author, although I frequently act like a powerless victim who has been unfairly and unwillingly inserted into a satirical comedy. I have the potential to affect the direction of my story, even if just attitudinally, which could alter the entire plot.

Though the setting and characters have often changed, I remain the protagonist. There are prominent characters, some of whom have been in my saga from the beginning, such as my family, and others who randomly appear as the settings change daily, weekly, monthly, or yearly. The plot often takes a turn without my input, but the theme can still stay the same regardless. Themes such as truth, perseverance, faith, love, family, friendship, or hope can remain in the most sinister of plots.

More interesting to me is the fact that we are all characters in the stories of others. We frequently tramp carelessly through life without regard for the role we are playing in the stories of those around us. Am I a confidante, antagonist, or static character? Are my lines carefully considered, as they would be if I (the co-author) were actually writing them? How would my character be described physically, emotionally, and spiritually? In which chapter do I appear on the scene in this person's story? Is it a period of conflict, resolution, or climax? Did I carefully exit the episode or thoughtlessly disappear, leaving the main character alone, afraid, angry, resentful, or sad? How would I respond to my character in the story? Would she infuriate or inspire me? Would I rationalize this character's actions the way I perhaps do in reality, or would I see more clearly the truth of my persona?

It's all a story, this life we live, and we are all participating in one grand story. Like it or not, we are characters in the stories of everyone we encounter daily, weekly, monthly, and yearly until death. There is a Divine Author who has written the one book that is common to all of our stories and who is reading each of our stories as they unfold. We've been given the job of a lifetime—co-author of this non-fiction. How would we feel if we could watch Him pick up our personal storybooks and begin to read? Would He smile with pride or gasp at our careless additions? We'll all find out in the epilogue.

*"In the beginning was the Word,
and the Word was with God,
and the Word was God."*

John 1:1

"Blessed are the pure in heart,
for they will see God."

Matthew 5:8

SEE NO EVIL

My heart was full of anxiety one night as I tried to process some information I'd received from a friend. A young woman hung herself and was in a coma. The very little I knew about this precious life was all I needed to know; she was sexually abused as a child. My friend and I were trying to come to terms with the injustice, sadness, and evil of it all. My usual disposition of optimism and hope was temporarily shattered. I was enraged and bewildered at the harm that human beings inflict upon others, we who are made in the image and likeness of God!

I scanned my brain for all of the answers that might come from my theological studies ... free will, the reality of evil, judgment day for the perpetrator, blah, blah, blah. The truth of the matter is that I was not going to hear anything that would console me at that moment unless God Himself came down to speak to me. There simply is no answer that will suffice, one that will make me say, "Oh, I get it. It's all fine now." No. It's not fine. In fact, sometimes it can seem unbearable.

We must each search our own heart, know ourselves, and be ourselves. In a world of darkness and lies, we *must* manifest light and truth. If we are all hiding in our own protective shells with secrets, shame, and pain, how can we possibly help each other heal? How can we come to recognize evil when we are uncertain of true goodness? Transparency is essential because evil prefers to be hidden. One by one we must emerge like shining crystal clear light bulbs charged by the energy that only God can provide. We cannot do it alone: we must unite in truth, love, and, hope.

Will we solve the world's problems and eliminate evil, strife, and pain? No, but we will feel the power of good, justice, truth, and hope. We will hold hands and walk together, protecting each other. Evil will soon no longer be able to deceive us. It will be the outcast, the one that is obscure, and we will shatter it before it shatters us. If doing so would alter one person's personal struggle, we will have won. We will realize the power of God.

"If any of you put a stumbling block
before one of these little ones
who believe in me,
it would be better for you
if a great millstone
were fastened around your neck
and you were drowned in
the depth of the sea."

Matthew 18:6

"For surely I know the plans
I have for you, says the Lord,
plans for your welfare and not for harm,
to give you a future with hope."

Jeremiah 29:11

HISTORY

My husband and I joined a new gym recently. It's a mid-sized, family-owned place that has plenty of aerobic equipment, weights, and some group classes. As I exercised, I noticed various posters throughout the facility. There were several of muscleman Arnold Schwarzenegger when he was very young, one each of the movies *Flashdance* and *Saturday Night Fever*, and a few others that brought me back to the 70s and 80s. I started to reminisce about those years and the celebrities who influenced me and set the exercise trends of the times. My husband has always been into lifting weights; while I bounced around from one fad to another — Jazzercise, kickboxing, step classes, aerobics, yoga, cycling, etc.

Several years ago, while doing Jazzercise, I talked with the instructor about the earlier days when we exercised barefoot with rather provocative spandex outfits, cut high at the thigh and complete with leg warmers (in case we got cold?). She responded, "I wasn't even born yet." Ouch! Then came the parachute pants and Reebok sneakers. Somewhere along the lines, I sported head and wristbands. Nowadays, it's yoga pants. Thank God for that, because nobody wants to see my middle-aged body in spandex and leg warmers!

As my mind wandered, I started to wonder what the trends of the future will be. Arnold and those steroid-abusing figures from the 70s and 80s fortunately don't seem to be in vogue these days, probably because many of those guys died young from the effects of the drugs on their hearts. Yet in their time, that was "in." I realized right then and there that I won't get to see the whole picture. I only get to see a small bit of the world's history during the brief period of time I am here. The things that are familiar to me will change, and I will not know how life changes, hopefully progresses, or how it all ends. I am only here for a brief part of the story.

It reminds me of the tale of the blind men who were placed around various parts of the elephant and then asked to describe it. Each man had a conflicting description because he was positioned at a different part of the elephant's body. Similarly, if you place five people at a window overlooking a scene, but from different floors of the same building, each will describe it differently. All are correct, but each one is different.

That's the way it is in life. We come and go, generation after generation, each getting a small glimpse and a different view because of the time we are on earth. If we had been born sooner or later, the "view" would be different.

I wonder what the exercise trends will be in the year 2100. How advanced will technology become? Will cancer be cured? Will pollution be a thing of the past? I will never know. In the epic book of world history, the time I live in is but a simple page. That's humbling. It makes me realize that the big picture, like the elephant or the building, is not going to be fully revealed to me here on my little page. I only see that which I can see from my position in time and space, and there is much more than meets these little eyes of mine.

In the grand scheme of things, it is not my story at all. It never was. It's HIStory.

Everything Has Its Time

For everything there is a season,
and a time for every matter under heaven:
a time to be born, and a time to die;
a time to plant, and
a time to pluck up what is planted;
a time to kill, and a time to heal;
a time to break down, and a time to build up;
a time to weep, and a time to laugh;
a time to mourn, and a time to dance;
a time to throw away stones, and
a time to gather stones together;
a time to embrace, and
a time to refrain from embracing;
a time to seek, and a time to lose;
a time to keep, and a time to throw away;
a time to tear, and a time to sew;
a time to keep silence, and a time to speak;
a time to love, and a time to hate;
a time for war, and a time for peace.

Ecclesiastes 3:1-8

The Balancing Act

Thomas Merton said, "Happiness is not a matter of intensity but of balance, order, rhythm and harmony." Sounds simple enough, right? I imagine it has never been easy to live a balanced life, but nowadays it seems especially hard. I remember a short vacation at the shore where my husband and I sat like two aging athletes who had just run ten consecutive marathons on a treadmill. I slept the entire first day, all the while insisting I must be terminally ill. We didn't want to do a thing except sit and stare blankly at the ocean in between bouts of unconsciousness. Our battered bodies seemed to absorb the sun, fresh ocean air, and gentle, cool breeze like malnourished plants.

It took us several days to unwind and settle our frantic minds and war-weary bodies, but once the shock wore off, we began to actually enjoy life. Imagine that! We went to breakfast and exercised in the morning, read books by the ocean in the afternoon, went for a picnic lunch by the bay, and walked the beach or boardwalk at night. We even had time to visit family. The sky seemed brighter, the people happier, and we felt much healthier. Life was good.

When Monday rolled around, we got back on that dreadful treadmill again. Everything seemed darker and faster, and the people are downright nasty. I was making phone calls and appointments, filling out endless paperwork, cooking, and cleaning, and Mark was commuting back and forth to the insanity of his downsizing company. Where was the sun and the breeze? Where did all the smiling people go? Why was my head killing me again?

Then one morning, I decided to open my windows instead of living with the constant buzzing of the air conditioner. I decided to make a picnic dinner for my family on the patio, complete with a red and white checkered tablecloth and lemonade in a glass pitcher. I was going to get off of that treadmill and balancing my life if it kills me!

I have a good visual hanging on my refrigerator. It's a simple pie chart divided into eight slices (I should probably change it to sixteen), and it has space for me to fill in to indicate which slice(s) of the pie I am setting aside for family, friends, work, spirituality, exercise, relaxation, entertainment, etc. When I do complete this chart, I am astounded to see how truly unbalanced my life is.

The thing about balance is that it doesn't just happen. Think about a balance ball, balance beam, or tightrope. Anything that requires balance requires awareness, concentration, effort, and a bit of skill, all of which entail effort. If I want to live a balanced life (and I desperately do!), I must work at the art of balance. I cannot stumble blindly through life like I am prey being dragged by a hungry lion. I have to rise with a purpose and a plan for the day, and I have to work at balancing that work. Each day should include time for prayer, meals, rest, exercise, work, family, friends, and self. That's no small task! It necessitates the awareness and inclusion of balance and order. Unlike the usual drudgery that depletes me, the work of balance and order will help me to thrive and will bring sunshine and gentle breezes into my daily routine.

*"Do not be conformed to this world,
but be transformed by
the renewing of your minds,
so that you may discern
what is the will of God—
what is good and acceptable and perfect."*

Romans 12:2

"Blessed are the peacemakers,
for they will be called children of God."

Matthew 5:9

Ignorance is Not Bliss

I went to see the movie *Selma* the first night it came out in my area. I was eager to learn more about Martin Luther King Jr., a man I knew so little about and yet admired so much. The movie left me feeling ashamed, ignorant, and yet strangely hopeful. It also jogged a few memories and shed new light on them, the light of truth.

I grew up in Newark, New Jersey in the 1960s and 70s. My dad was a fireman in our city, and he worked a few other part-time jobs to support his wife and four children. We were rather poor. Initially, we lived in a five-family house in which each of the families had anywhere from one to four kids. The neighborhood was a mixture of all white, second-generation immigrants, the majority being Italian and Irish. My siblings and I walked to the public school we attended (initially all white), swam in the local community pool, and played in the streets of our all-white neighborhood. We really had no idea of the mounting civil rights issues of the times. That's remarkable because we lived in a large city during monumental moments in the history of civil rights, including the Civil Rights Act (1964), the Voting Rights Act (1965), the Newark riots (1967), the Fair Housing Act (1968), the 1971 school desegregation through mandatory busing, and more.

Yet, I don't recall being taught any of this in school. All I knew is what I heard from the kids around me: "They are going to be busing *them* into our schools, so we have to switch schools; the neighborhood is changing so we have to move," etc. Forty-some-odd years later, I'm just now learning that it was all exceedingly biased and all too similar to the scenes in the movie *Selma*.

As I sat watching the silent marches in the movie, a particular memory was sparked. One day while playing outside, I observed what must have been thousands of African Americans marching silently up the avenue. The unified group spanned from each side of the avenue and as far down as I could see. It was a powerful and unnerving sight, but I had no idea what was happening. The word on the street was "They are claiming the neighborhood. We all have to move." I am ashamed to say that this is what I thought and believed all of these years until I saw *Selma*. I don't know the exact year, but I'm guessing I was about ten-years-old — old enough to have been educated about civil rights, and yet I wasn't.

While watching the film, I cried at the injustice, smiled at the unity, marveled at the bravery, and was angered by the ignorance — the ignorance of people who were uneducated, fearful (of what I'll never know), and part of the problem instead of part of the solution. I'm disgusted with the officials in charge of the education system, the political leaders, scout leaders, Church leaders, and anyone else who should have known better and led children like myself towards truth, justice, peace, and solidarity.

When I left the theater, I couldn't help but wonder why Martin Luther King Jr. was not declared a saint. He was a faithful, peaceful, brilliant, zealous, compassionate, and dedicated man who devoted his all-too-short life seeking and working towards a peaceful resolution to a problem that was blatantly unjust. Meanwhile, saints have been canonized who fought for justice in far less dignified ways. Could the reason be because he was not a Catholic Christian? When will we learn? I'll be praying to Saint Martin Luther King Jr., and I know he'll hear me.

Then the Lord God said,
"It is not good that
the man should be alone;
I will make him
a helper as his partner."

Genesis 2:18

What's Your Instinct?

My dog Snoopy has major psychological issues. He's been a basket case his whole life. Whenever we leave the house, he goes into a panic. He yelps and cries as soon as he sees any hint of a possibility that we are leaving. At first it was cute; "Look how much he loves us! He doesn't want us to leave." It wasn't long, however, before we were hollering, "Shut up, Snoopy!" and racing to the door, eager to close it behind us to shut out his annoying howling.

When we came back home (whether in two minutes or two hours), it was certain that there would be a lovely present for us. Some type of excretion was inevitable. In addition, we've been greeted with ripped up papers of every kind (including money); torn apart pens, pencils, plastic containers and/or bags; and ripped apart stuffed animals and pillows. He even figured out how to open the refrigerator, eating anything within his reach and leaving the container on the living room floor for us.

Eventually, after the destruction of several important items and finally tiring of the surprises and unplanned cleaning and mopping sessions, we started crating him whenever we left the house. He barked and howled the entire time we were gone (to the point of being hoarse), whether it was two hours or twelve hours. The poor thing. The poor neighbors! We were at a loss as to what to do with him.

Then, my daughter's cat Romeo came to stay with us for a while. Guess what? Snoopy is as quiet as a mouse when we leave. When we come home, there are no surprises. Well, actually, it's a huge surprise to discover nothing awaiting us except Snoopy and Romeo happily standing side-by-side at the door.

All he needed was a friend. The loneliness was killing the poor guy! I should have known, as the feeling is not foreign to me. It's no fun being alone in the house, and I have the ability to leave whenever I want to escape the isolation. What about the sick or elderly? What about those who don't drive? What about those suffering from social anxiety or phobias? It can be a living hell. If others are not paying attention or reading our signals correctly, the suffering can continue for years unnecessarily.

Mother Teresa was exposed to severe poverty, yet she said: "The most terrible poverty is loneliness, and the feeling of being unloved." Snoopy had that figured out long before I did. He just needed a friend to sit with him.

There's a lesson there for all of us. Most of us don't outwardly express our needs the way Snoopy did. Perhaps we're too proud. However, we all have a need to be loved, to be with others, and to be held and praised. Animals aren't as "intelligent" as us. They are driven by instinct. Yet sometimes I think we're too "smart" for our own good.

Then the Lord God said, "It is not good that the man should be alone; I will make him a helper as his partner."

Genesis 2:18

"So if anyone is in Christ,
there is a new creation:
everything old has passed away;
see, everything has become new!"

2 Corinthians 5:17

Death and New Life

Years ago, I wrote a reflection about death and dying titled *Death Becomes Us*. I basically said that we live our best lives in the constant awareness of death, because it is then that we take nothing for granted. I'm a bit older now and that much closer to death. I'm also in the midst of watching my eleven-year-old beagle lose the function of his hind legs. My sister is struggling with late-stage breast cancer. My friend watched her husband die from brain cancer. My parents are elderly and not in the best of health. I have to tell you…I definitely do not feel like I'm living my best life in this constant awareness of death. I can't help but wonder, is this some kind of cruel joke or something?

It has always freaked me out a bit, the fact that someday I will cease to exist. I asked my husband this evening what is going to happen to Snoopy. He has suddenly aged quite rapidly. He can't hear, can't walk, and can't seem to wake up from his very deep slumbers. My husband said something like, "He will just die, like our bird did years ago. He will just fall over and die or never wake up." I have been extremely fortunate because thus far I have not had to watch a human loved one suffer and die, but if my reaction to my parakeet years ago is any indication of my response, I'm in big trouble over here.

I remember the day vividly. I was cooking rice pudding in the commercial kitchen in my home where I had a food manufacturing business. My co-worker Wendy was with me, as always. We were going about the usual routine when I suddenly heard a *plop*. My parakeet Honey had been ill, and I knew that sound was coming from the direction of his cage. I stopped everything and stared at Wendy. "I think Honey died," I said and went into a panic. I asked Wendy to go into the room and check because there was no way I could handle the sight of my beloved bird dead on the bottom of the cage. Wendy went in and confirmed my fatal assumption. She kindly put a towel over the cage and removed it from the house, while I proceeded to mourn instantaneously. My little feathered friend who sat on my shoulders and kissed my cheek for over ten years was now lifeless at the bottom of his cage. I ask you, how on earth am I going to handle a human death?

Beyond the concern of the dreaded grieving process is just the gnawing question of the meaning of it all. These beings — human and otherwise — that we are and experience life with simply must be more than matter. "We are dust and to dust we shall return" is actually a hope-filled statement, because dust in the cosmos is in a constant state of conversion and renewal. Likewise, dead and decaying organisms contribute greatly to the carbon cycle in a process that generates energy and life.

These are scientific facts that speak to the intellect and seem to somehow make sense, albeit their miraculous process. Everything seems to point to death followed by new life. Each new day, season, and year are reminders of the process of endings and new beginnings. St. Paul knew that long before modern science affirmed it. He said: ". . . just as Christ was raised from the dead by the glory of the Father, so we too might walk in newness of life" (Romans 6:4). It's a promise that not only comforts me but gives meaning to life, death, and suffering and great hope for my high-spirited soul.

> *"The Lord is my strength and my shield; in him my heart trusts; so I am helped, and my heart exults, and with my song I give thanks to him."*
>
> **Psalm 28:7**

Distinguishing the Giver and the Gifts

Childbirth is an awesome miracle to experience, and I remember vividly the birth of my two daughters (three and a half years apart). My husband and I were a young couple given the responsibility of caring for two perfect, precious beings with ten little fingers and ten little toes. They looked so peaceful when they slept in the hospital crib and so angry when they cried! When the nurse wrapped our firstborn and placed her in my arms to bring home, I looked up at her with fearful eyes. I had no idea what to do with this child, but the nurse seemed to be under the false impression that I did. Fortunately, it turned out that motherhood and fatherhood are innate. We couldn't help but love and cherish these babies with every ounce of our being, and they became the center of our world.

Watching them grow was fun and exciting. I recall taking the girls as babies and toddlers to church and gazing lovingly at them throughout the entire Mass, admittedly focusing way more on the children than on the words of the priest. They truly were gifts from God, and we simply could not get over the blessing and miracle. Every adorable gesture they made brought a smile to our faces. We loved, nurtured, nourished, educated, and spent quality time with them as all good parents do, to the point perhaps that they became little gods to us. We would do anything for them.

The Principle and Foundation of St. Ignatius' Spiritual Exercises explains that "all the things in this world are gifts of God presented to us so that we can know God more easily . . . but if any of these gifts become the center of our lives, they displace God and so hinder our growth toward our goal." It took me many years to realize that those words refer to all people, places, and things on this earth — including my children. How difficult it is for a mom to let go of her children and cling to and trust in God! It was and remains the most difficult task of my life.

I often think of Abraham's trust in God as he placed Isaac on the altar. I have had to do that metaphorically many times with my daughters. The first time I screamed in anger at God. How dare He give me this gift and ask me to return it? I felt betrayed, and I absolutely lacked trust.

I am grateful for the reminder that the curses I encounter can be blessings if I respond in ways that will save my soul, because it is for that purpose that I am here on this earth — "to praise, reverence, and serve God . . . and by means of this to save [my] soul." Just as I should have focused on God during the Mass when my girls were babies, now too I must remember to turn my gaze towards God. My life, soul, and salvation rest upon the foundation of God — nothing and no one else.

"I am with you always,
to the end of the age."

Matthew 28:20

Now You See It...
Now You Don't

I was thinking today about how easily something can become nothing. Those things that we value so much on this earth, such as our homes, clothes, jewelry, electronics, people, jobs, and even our own bodies, can quickly become obsolete. This is, of course, only natural. Things that we can feel, taste, touch, and hear surround us. They are reminders of our material existence, and they are within our physical reach, so we place a high value on them. It's all too easy because it's right there in front of us for the taking, kind of like the opposite of the old adage, "Out of sight, out of mind." Usually it's more like "Close in sight and close in mind." However, these things that are in our sight can be taken from us in an instant. Where then do we turn?

This idea came to my mind as a number of friends recently called me quite upset about the transfer of several local, beloved priests. They are physical reminders of God's presence, and they act "In Persona Christi," so it's only natural that people are drawn to them. We all want a piece of God, a living, tangible, earthly piece of an otherwise invisible God whom we so desperately need. We reach out in so many childlike ways grasping desperately to fill this void. When someone (or something) seems to quench that insatiable thirst, we cling to it and are temporarily satisfied. We think we have found the missing piece. We are safe.

Then suddenly, the physical reminder disappears, or the thing that we are using to fill the thirst no longer quenches, and we are once again left in our own desperation. This is a frightening and lonely place that we prefer to run from, to the arms of another person, place, or thing so that we don't have to sit there in our own nothingness. Please, someone, something, fill this void! The discomfort, pain, emptiness, loneliness and awareness of my complete and utter powerlessness is all too real. I must regain control.

Here in this place of fear and uncertainty is a gift, because in that place is God. We can't purchase this gift; we rarely even hear of it. We can't see it, smell it, touch it, taste it, or hear it (not physically anyway), so we might not trust it. How can this thing, which isn't a tangible thing, do anything at all to quench my earthly body? How can it hold me, comfort me, counsel me, and feed me? Most of us cannot sit there long enough to discover that it absolutely can and does. "It" has a name and is more real than anything or anyone we could ever come into contact with on earth. He is eternal. He is omnipotent. He is "with us always, even to the end of time."

True joy and freedom come when we stop running from ourselves, when we release those material things that give us a false sense of security. It is when we surrender people, places, and things and enter into ourselves that we discover the one and only reality that will never leave us. If we lose all those people and things around us, and even our own physical abilities, He will still remain. We are safer than we could ever imagine, if we only stop running.

> *"Now the whole earth had one language and the same words."*
>
> **Genesis 11:1**

One Language

I once went on a tour of Italy with a group of people from around the world. There were about forty people ranging in age from twenty to eighty, and from my calculation, at least ten countries were represented. It was admittedly a bit peculiar and uncomfortable at first as we ate dinner and mingled with strangers. I somehow felt that I had to be more cognizant of my own habits and customs. I wondered if my way of greeting people, dining at table, or even conversing might seem odd or offensive. It was a feeling that made me want to separate myself from the group and retreat to that familiar place of comfort alone with my husband. Fortunately, I did not succumb to that initial temptation.

It wasn't long at all before my thoughts were replaced by the warm presence of my travel companions. From the initial introductions when people briefly told stories of why they were on this tour, a sense of camaraderie was forming. That dream of traveling to new and beautiful places is universal, as is the deep desire to fulfill that lifelong dream before death. I listened as people from opposite ends of the earth shared the events that brought them to this tour at this particular time in their lives. The anticipation, hope, and excitement were common traits from day one. I think most of us also had an underlying fear that annoying or inconsiderate group members could possibly ruin this important trip. That hidden sense of caution and self-protection was also present early on, I think.

The wariness waned very quickly. *My* trip soon became *our* trip, and I truly believe that each and every person wanted to see the others' dreams fulfilled in the way that they imagined. The nationalities, languages, and accents became replaced by one language — human. It's a language without words, but speaks more clearly, boldly, and influentially than any other. It's a language that defies age, education, location, and religion. This universal language takes the form of laughter, dancing, sadness, fear, concern, love, beauty, awe, mystery, joy, kinship, and protection. It's soul. It's heart speaking to heart. It's beautiful, and it's universal.

Look at the person next to you when you are stuck at a traffic light, sitting on a bus, or in a waiting room or restaurant. Find the person in the crowd that looks *least* like you or the person who does not speak your language. It might be the person who is covered from head to toe in a scarf or the homeless person who hasn't bathed in days. Take a second look at the neighbor who is your enemy or the teacher who berates you. Then look past everything that you see outwardly and look deep within. There you will find the human soul — the same one that is within you. Connect with it. You will recognize it instantly, and it will nourish you — with or without words.

"Whoever does not love does not know God, for God is love."

1 John 4:8

The Divine Weaver
Author Unknown

My life is but a weaving
Between my Lord and me;
I cannot choose the colors
He weaves so steadily.
Often He weaves in sorrow
But I in foolish pride
Forget He sees the upper
And I, the lower side.
But the dark threads are as needful
In the weaver's skillful hand
As the threads of gold and silver
In the pattern He has planned.
Not till the loom is silent
And the bobbins cease to fly,
Shall He unroll the canvas
And explain the reason why.

Life Tightly Woven

Throughout the course of my graduate education in spirituality, I came to examine my life from various perspectives. For example, one semester I had to create a tapestry of my life, and in another, we were asked to reflect upon and tell the story of our lives. If that assignment had been due recently, it would have said, "Life is fragile and can fall apart at the seams at any moment." I sometimes cannot believe the twists and turns of life, and lately it seems to be unraveling at the speed of sound. My life, however, is more than a fragile piece of porcelain dangling on a ledge that can shatter into a million pieces.

The tapestry analogy gives me great hope. When I was a little girl, I had one of those toy weaving looms that came with a plastic bag filled with colorful bands of yarn, a wooden needle, and other tools that aided in pushing and pulling the yarn deliberately into place on the loom. I enjoyed the tedious and intricate work of choosing a particular pattern first, then selecting the colors of yarn, setting them on the loom one piece at a time, and weaving each piece over and under the other threads until I reached the other side of the loom. This process was carefully repeated until the project was complete, and voila, I had created either a potholder or a scarf or some other such item. Whatever the finished product, it was sturdy; tightly woven, and it would not come apart unless it was intentionally unwoven. More importantly, it could not come apart while it was being woven because it was on the loom in the weaving process.

I've got to believe that my life's tapestry undergoes a similar process by the Divine Weaver. I can't really say that it can "come apart at the seams at any moment" because it's still on the loom, and it will remain there until my life is over. The twists and turns that make me feel as if life is fragile and falling apart are simply new pieces of yarn that are being interwoven with the other yarn. It's a tedious process, and I will not be able to see the end result in my lifetime, because the tapestry of my life is in the weaving process that is life. As long as I am alive, the weaving will continue. My faith, however, tells me to trust the weaver. He's quite skillful.

> *"Pride goes before destruction,
> and a haughty spirit before a fall."*
>
> Proverbs 16:18

Foolish Pride

I find it somewhat comforting to know that Adam and Eve succumbed to temptation while they were living in a pristine garden, naked, joyful, and free with access to lush, pure vegetation and direct contact with God. I mean, I've got a lot of good excuses compared to them, right? Picture the birds flitting, the livestock roaming, the rivers rolling, and the pleasant conversations between Adam, Eve, and God. No text messages, employment issues, relationship disputes, health problems, or financial concerns — just Adam, Eve, and God. Nothing troublesome existed to cause angst until the snake slithered onto the scene just to ruin the fun.

The snake (Satan) pointed out to Adam and Eve that they were being tyrannized because God didn't want them to be as powerful as He. Perhaps Adam and Eve wanted God's power, or maybe they simply felt betrayed by God and couldn't stand to think that they were possibly being deceived by Him. They were afraid to trust God because it could mean (if they were in fact being deceived) that their egos would be bruised. It was an attachment to the self and a refusal to risk being found fools.

By contrast, you've got Abraham who marched quite confidently up to the top of the mountain, tied up his only son, stacked some wood, and was all set to offer him up as a sacrifice because God asked him to do so. He had no fears about being foolish and look what he was about to do!

While we can't imagine a literal burnt human offering, I do think it's sometimes easier to sacrifice the people we love than it is to surrender our own pride, so strong is the cement that bonds the brick walls of our hearts. We would rather let go of people and abandon our relationships than hurt our own pride. It takes a great deal of courage and faith in ourselves and in God to stand vulnerably in the light, naked and exposed to possible harm to our egos.

We are faced with these options daily — cling to our pride or relinquish our attachment to it. Adam and Eve show us that we have to become aware of the meandering voice within that tries to manipulate us with its lies. We learn from them the deep, lasting, and wide-ranging pain that befalls us when we choose to cling to our egos and hide in shame behind our own fear. Abraham teaches us the positive, albeit arduous work of surrender. It's uphill, uncomfortable, and takes commitment, determination, courage and a heck of a lot of faith, but the fruits of it are "as numerous as the stars of heaven" (Genesis 26:4).

*"The haughty eyes of people
shall be brought low,
and the pride of everyone
shall be humbled;
and the Lord alone will be
exalted on that day."*

Isaiah 2:11

"Hear this, O Job;
stop and consider
the wondrous works of God."

Job 37:14

Still Learning to Be

I am an artist, but ever since I was a little girl, I can only draw what I see directly in front of me. I cannot create from my imagination. Until reading about contemplation for class, I truly had no idea why this annoyance plagued me. After reading Jesuit theologian Walter Burghardt's article, *A Long, Loving Look at the Real*, I realized that I cannot retrieve images from my memory because I do not look long enough at anything to remember it. I am sad to say that my life is the antithesis of contemplation. I have joined the ranks of the majority in America and have become a human doing rather than the human being I was born to be. Considering my artistic dilemma goes back to my childhood, I have a feeling this has been the case since then.

Six years ago, my husband and I went to Ireland for our twenty-fifth wedding anniversary. It was a dream that I'd had for many, many years. We rented a car and drove all around that beautiful island for seven days. It was everything I hoped it would be, but I didn't know how to savor it. We drove from town to town, from one exquisite scene to another, snapping photos and moving on to the next place. One day we went to the Cliffs of Mohr. We drove for hours in anticipation to get there. When we finally parked at the top of the Cliffs, we looked for a few moments and then said, "Okay, now what do we do?!" There was nothing to "do" there — only to see. We took a few photos and moved on within minutes from a place I had longed to be half of my life because I didn't know what I was supposed to "do" there. I didn't know how to enjoy "a long, loving look at the real." If I did, I might have had an image in my memory to paint when I returned home.

This dilemma of not looking and seeing is not the only indicator of my non-contemplative life. I have difficulty "wasting" time in play. I do not enjoy festivities at all because I have always felt guilty just relaxing when I could be doing something productive instead.

I'm certain there are plenty of psychological theories that could explain my behavior; however, I have already begun the practice of undoing the damage. Soon after this reflection, as I sat out on my balcony with a book, I heard some geese honking overhead. It took me a few minutes to remember to stop and look up, but I finally did and noticed beautiful flocks of geese flying in wild V formations so close that I could distinguish the black wings and white bellies! I just looked — long and lovingly — and I even have the image in my mind to draw. Imagine that!

"Open my eyes, so that I may behold wondrous things out of your law."

Psalm 119:18

"In the beginning when God created
the heavens and the earth,
the earth was a formless void
and darkness covered the face of the deep,
while a wind from God
swept over the face of the waters.
Then God said, 'Let there be light';
and there was light.
And God saw that the light was good;
and God separated
the light from the darkness.
God called the light Day,
and the darkness he called Night.
And there was evening
and there was morning, the first day."

Genesis 1:1-5

Day and Night

Don't ask me why, but one morning I woke up at 2 AM wondering about the mysteries of good and evil. (I know what you're thinking, but I've already tried medication.) I was probably subconsciously pondering a discussion I'd had with a friend who (not unlike me) was going through some very wearisome circumstances in her life right then. We talked until bedtime about the calamities of life that can seem downright intolerable, and we wondered (like most people do) why such difficulties keep occurring. When will life just become peaceful and joy-filled for at least a six-month period? Why does life have to be so awful sometimes?

As I sat in the dark in my office, I recalled my thoughts about Adam and Eve in "Foolish Pride." I remembered reading how "in the beginning . . . darkness was over the surface of the deep," and the light had to be separated from the darkness. It occurred to me that the light and the dark (the good and the bad) exist concurrently and have since the beginning. In fact, according to the story, it was darkness that first loomed over the earth before God produced the light and divided it from the dark. He didn't eliminate it; He divided it. So many good and beautiful things lived and flourished between the day and the night, but the night remained with glimmers of smaller light always present to "govern the night." Never was it decided that there should not be darkness again, but rather that the two should be separated, and the light (no matter how small) would always rule. Then I recalled the crucifixion — the epitome of hell on earth existing simultaneously with heaven on earth.

That which seems excruciating and intolerable exists in unison with love and peace.

These opposing and contradictory forces, heaven and hell (darkness and light) do not collide and explode. They coexist, and the light always guides the dark if we let it. What a valuable lesson! I must remember that there has always and will always be times of darkness and light — day and night — and all of those moments that occur in between (dusk, dawn, twilight, etc.). To expect or wait for times without darkness is to hope for something that has never existed since before Creation. The trick is to let the darkness be without constantly disputing it (a futile practice) and to notice the light (no matter how small) that is always present, flickering, and guiding us through even the darkest nights.

*"For once you were darkness,
but now in the Lord you are light.
Live as children of light —
for the fruit of the light is found
in all that is good and right and true."*

Ephesians 5:8-9

"I came that they may have life,
and have it abundantly."

John 10:10

Open to Receive

Once, my husband and I drove to Chicago from Pennsylvania. I really don't like driving long distances, but it beats the alternative of flying. Most of the drive was smooth, relaxing, and carefree. I read while my husband drove, and he worked on his laptop when I drove. We averaged about eighty miles per hour in sunny or at least fair weather on a long, clear, wide, and mostly well-maintained stretch of highway. We talked, ate, and were generally cheerful most of the trip. It was a twelve-hour drive, but we stopped one night in each direction to make for a more relaxing and enjoyable trip.

One day on the ride home, the GPS told us to get off at an exit that did not coincide with the signs overhead, which pointed east. We hesitated for a second (couldn't pause too long at that rate of speed), and then my husband made the decision to remain on the highway and follow the signs overhead instead of the voice on the GPS. Within one minute, our speed slowed to a halt, and we were stuck in a single lane in bumper-to-bumper traffic spanning as far as the eye could see.

I'm not one to just sit there and acknowledge my powerlessness in a situation like that. Immediately, my brain started scanning the possibilities. Were we too far from the exit that the GPS told us to take? Yep. Could we drive along the shoulder to the next exit? Nope. There was physically no way out, so I started subconsciously seeking emotional reprieve. Blame was the obvious first tool — it was all my husband's fault. Didn't I tell him to listen to the GPS? Anger came next. Why are they doing construction in the middle of the day when people are traveling? Why can't they do this stuff at night? Fear followed. What if I have to go to the bathroom? What would I do if I was even five years older in this situation? The bladder doesn't cooperate the way it used to, you know. Meanwhile, as my thoughts darted from idea to idea, my frustration and temper increased. There seemed to be no way out — neither out of the traffic nor my escalating emotional chaos.

As you probably have figured out, acceptance does not come easily to me. It feels like defeat, and I'm a fighter. Acceptance, however, is actually far from defeat. It's living in reality. Acceptance is defined as "the act of taking or receiving something." In the example of my traffic dilemma, I had to simply sit back and take and receive the moment, as uncomfortable as it was. I tried everything else first (my typical pattern), but it wasn't until I accepted the reality of the situation and allowed it to simply be that I could come to a place of peace, free from the inner turmoil. It's so simple — taking and receiving — yet so difficult.

When the twists and turns of life go in the directions that I think they should, I'm all about acceptance. When things do not go the way I think they should, I enter into a state of resistance and refusal in the same way that I did in the traffic jam. I start to blame God for all the unpleasant and uncomfortable things that are happening either to me or around me. I become angry. I seek emotional reprieve. I live in a state of fear.

Life is a gift that was given to me. To accept that gift fully, I need to receive all that it has to offer — the joy, the sorrow, the fear, the good, and the bad. To be truly in acceptance, I must be willing to experience the pain that comes just as I am willing to accept the joy. I must accept the traffic jams along with the wide-open highways. It's a posture of openness to receive the gift that was given without putting conditions on my willingness to receive. The actions that we take to free ourselves from reality do not free us from the pain. They merely mask it temporarily, and they hinder our growth, drawing us in the opposite direction of the One who gave us the gift.

Don't run. Draw nearer. Be open to receive all of it.

"Now I appeal to you, brothers and sisters, by the name of our Lord Jesus Christ, that all of you be in agreement and that there be no divisions among you, but that you be united in the same mind and the same purpose."

1 Corinthians 1:10

Worthy of Love

I met with a woman in the hospital recently. She is a beautiful, young, intelligent person — a loving mother and a beloved daughter. Like tens of thousands of others in America, she is caught in the grips of the opioid epidemic and was briefly hospitalized after an overdose. We talked for a bit and discussed the hardships of recovery and the treatment industry. Her family groped for help from the hospital and others who might be able to guide them to a safe place for healing and hope. Several days later, she was found unconscious (OD) in a parking lot after being released prematurely from the hospital to a recovery house, where she was forced to wander the streets daily looking for work. The injustices are too many to list in this brief reflection.

She is unreachable these days, but I sent her a private message encouraging her to never give up. Among other things, I wrote: "you are worthy." Afterward, I thought about the implications of the word "worthy," so I looked up the definition. It is defined as "deserving effort, attention, or respect - good enough." I wonder, who is it that judges if someone is good enough? Who decides which people are deserving of attention or respect? How and why could anyone suffering from an affliction feel less than deserving of love, attention, hope, and healing? What is our obligation to others in making them feel worthy? It's not something we can give to ourselves, because we see our reflections, as in a mirror, through the eyes of others.

I believe that we are all innately good people who often become misguided. We might make judgments because we truly believe that we know what is right for another or what is best for the world. These human tendencies have been occurring since the beginning of the Church (and surely since the beginning of time). St. Paul's letters to the community in Corinth reveal similar propensities as people judged each other and were divided by their ethical and religious beliefs, education, and even by their feelings of spiritual superiority. It was bedlam in the name of Christ.

Paul reminds the community that anything they have in life is a gift that has been given to them by the Spirit, and that gift is to be used for the service of others — never to exalt themselves in holiness. If they don't use their gifts to serve others, the gifts are useless. He reminds the community (and us) that we are all connected, and everything we do affects someone. He tells them to "pursue love" (1 Corinthians 14:1).

Let's pursue love. Let's use our gifts for the service of others. Let's let our eyes be mirrors radiating love so that all who see their reflection in our eyes may feel worthy, because they are.

*"Then the father said to him,
'Son, you are always with me,
and all that is mine is yours.
But we had to celebrate and rejoice,
because this brother of yours was dead
and has come to life;
he was lost and has been found.'"*

Luke 15:31-32

"They shall be like a tree planted by water,
sending out its roots by the stream.
It shall not fear when heat comes,
and its leaves shall stay green;
in the year of drought it is not anxious,
and it does not cease to bear fruit."

Jeremiah 17:8

Lessons from a Tree

The term "aging gracefully" sounds like an oxymoron to me, at least at first glance and especially for women in American culture. Grace, in this context, has something to do with elegance, beauty, charm, ease, or naturalness. It denotes an appealing quality.

It's a lovely thought, the aging gracefully thing, but so far in my experience, there is nothing beautiful, easy, or elegant about it, at least biologically.

I think trees can teach us something about aging gracefully. As the years go by, they grow taller and thicker, qualities that only make them sturdier. Their roots stretch further in all directions, growing deeper into the soil, where they grasp tightly to the nurturing earth that sustains them and gives them an unwavering strength. Likewise, the branches too grow denser and extend in many directions, allowing the atmosphere to nourish them. The powerful forces of the wind lift and carry the leaves in such ways that only magnify their beauty. The trunks become gnarled, a quality that somehow only commands even more respect from the observer. In short, an aged tree's very presence humbles a mindful person with its mighty and exquisite nobility.

In my neck of the woods where we women reside, aging doesn't seem to elicit thoughts of might and nobility. Instead, we shrink and shrivel, and any thickness we obtain is certainly not a desired or admired quality. Unlike trees, our physical presence seems to incur much less respect as we mature.

Yet if I look beyond the biological (and beyond the unhealthy and unnatural messages of American society), the analogy of the trees actually *is* quite descriptive of me. I'm a force to be reckoned with as I age. My soul is strong and solid. I've got roots that run deep, branches that reach to the heavens, and a spirit that is absolutely and positively magnified in powerful and beautiful ways against the forces of even devastating gale force winds.

Surprisingly, I'm even more capable now of bearing fruit than I was in my child-bearing years — the fruits of the Spirit! The fruits of the Spirit are love, joy, peace, patience, kindness, generosity, faithfulness, gentleness, and self-control (Galatians 5:22-23). Saint Paul said, "there is no law against such things" (Galatians 5:23). How right he was! The unwritten rules of this world and society are no match for those within the realm of the heart, where the tree of life resides and ages even more gracefully than the trees of this earth.

> *"We know that all things work together for good for those who love God, who are called according to his purpose."*
>
> **Romans 8:28**

Loosen Up

There are days when I believe a rubber band is the best analogy for my human existence. It often seems like I'm being emotionally pushed, pulled, stretched, twisted, and even warped in every possible direction. Within any given day, I sometimes feel like I experience more polar extremes than Antarctica. On those days, I sense a tension between the adverse emotional and spiritual forces that is confusing and quite uncomfortable: for example, living in both joy and sorrow at the same time.

Tension typically has negative implications. Whether we are referring to physical, emotional, spiritual, or relational tension, there is rarely a positive connotation. Tension is defined as "stretching or straining," which, like the usual association, sounds excruciating. It signifies pain, distress, or stretching — like a rubber band. By this definition, one would think tension should be avoided at all costs.

Yet when I hung my shower curtain on a tension rod a few days ago, I realized the audacious strength of its tautness as it is balanced, suspended and supported all at the same time. There is no apparent strain; rather, it appears solid and secure as it simultaneously presses and grips firmly from one side of the room to the other. It effortlessly carries the delicate curtain from top to bottom and side to side, allowing the curtain to dangle loosely from the tension rod's unyielding grip.

This observation reveals a tension in the meaning of the word itself. Tension can be defined and experienced as an imbalance or a counterbalance. Maybe it's as simple as how we choose to define it. Perhaps it requires a shift in perspective in tense situations. Do I choose to view myself and my experiences like the rubber band or the tension rod? Am I really being stretched, twisted, and warped, or am I being lengthened and strengthened?

I doubt my life will ever be free of tension. For example, there will always be forces pulling me towards experiences of and choices between work and play, self and other, good and evil, and joy and sorrow (and many other extremes in between). I can't escape the tension; it's built into the very fabric of life, even at the atomic level where it creates energy. What I can do is recognize that I have the choice to view my tense circumstances as either painful curses or counterbalances to the many blessings that I have received simultaneously. Like the tension rod which provides a strength and a harmony, my delicate soul is effortlessly carried in God's unyielding grip.

*"Do not fear, for I am with you,
do not be afraid, for I am your God;
I will strengthen you, I will help you,
I will uphold you
with my victorious right hand."*

Isaiah 41:10

"In the same way, let your light
shine before others,
so that they may see your good works
and give glory to your Father in heaven."

Matthew 5:16

Let Your Light Shine

Prayer is a powerful, noble, and necessary thing. We pray to worship, express our gratitude, petition, and bless. We pray for fortitude, courage, and the gifts of the Spirit, and I believe that our prayers are heard. Without prayer, we fumble through life by our own accord and eventually discover that we cannot sustain ourselves. It may not happen until our dying day, but I believe that ultimately we realize what we have been missing. Let's be honest though — we don't always know if our prayers are fruitful. We don't necessarily feel anything in return.

A few chapters ago, I wrote about the light and the dark without realizing how black the night can become. The very night I wrote that reflection originally, my daughter ended up in the ICU for nearly a week. Well-meaning friends sent text messages that read, "I'm praying for you and your family." I responded to one saying, "I cannot feel it." I never once questioned or doubted God's presence. I never once considered, "Why me?" Still, I searched desperately for a glimmer of light like the ones I wrote about, but I could not feel or see it, though many were praying.

The glimmers in the darkness came through people who chose to not only pray, but also to put the fruits of that prayer into some action that I could experience and feel. The light came through a neighbor who cooked meals for us when we couldn't even find the strength or energy to consider eating, much less cooking. There was more than a flicker shining through the hands of the nurses who so tenderly cared for my daughter. I felt its soft glow when friends visited the hospital and others spent time with me to try to normalize complicated and turbulent days. A ray came through several warm and very genuine long hugs. A glint could be felt in the gentle, empathetic ears of those who made themselves available to simply listen. Then on a day when I thought I could not get out of bed, someone who went to grammar school with my daughter contacted me with her mom and gave us a Christmas offering to help pay for expenses. I saw and felt hope in the people who brought the light into action in my darkness.

In all honesty, I don't know that I would have done any of those things that people did for me. That's one of the many graces that comes through times of strife. We grow in compassion. It's the ultimate paradox of life and one truth I can proclaim without hesitation. Like the purification process of gold, the fire transforms us and molds us into something more precious than before. It's the way our hearts become bright and beautiful like gold.

Once we've been transformed — once we've prayed and received the light — it's so important to bring the light into the darkness so that others can feel its radiant warmth. What good is light that is hidden? "No one after lighting a lamp puts it in a cellar, but on the lampstand so that those who enter may see the light" (Luke 11:33). I am so grateful to those who chose to bring their light into my world where it could be felt and for the lesson I received that I must do the same.

> *"Do not fear, for I am with you,*
> *do not be afraid, for I am your God;*
> *I will strengthen you, I will help you,*
> *I will uphold you*
> *with my victorious right hand."*
>
> **Isaiah 41:10**

At the End of Tears

At the end of tears is an unfamiliar place I have been reluctant to reach.

At the end of tears
it is calm.
It is quiet.
It is dark.
It is bright.
It is life —
a life that somehow remains although I tried to wash it away.
At the end of tears is a voice that whispers
I am here
and
you are here
and
it's okay.
Be still.
Do not be afraid.

"The light shines in the darkness,
and the darkness did not overcome it."

John 1:5

The Test of Faith

I've studied theology academically for about six years. I've read, contemplated, and written about the theology of suffering at various times throughout those years. It was fun, interesting, and intellectually stimulating. Experiencing its true meaning has been excruciating, on the other hand. The talk of faith is certainly much easier than the sometimes-crippling walk of faith, but what good is all the learning if I am unwilling or cannot pass a test? My most important and fruitful faith lessons continue to come, not through professors and books, but through the agonizing lessons of life that seem to advance in difficulties as I advance in stage.

Think about the simple, happy days in elementary school, the complications of high school, the rigors of college, and the challenges of graduate school. My faith education has progressed in a similar manner from simple, happy days to some very real challenges, which, in retrospect, were all necessary and appropriate for each particular stage. Like the difficult tests, lengthy papers, and demanding projects in college, my more advanced tests of faith have frequently been quite painful. Sure, there were times of guidance that came through grace-filled moments of peaceful prayer and experiences of enlightenment in joyful periods in my early days of learning, but education typically becomes more difficult as we advance. We expect that, right?

Throughout life's challenges, many have attempted to point me towards my faith for support. Someone specifically reminded me about my religion's teachings and my theological education on the redemptive value of suffering. It felt a bit like Charlie Brown's teacher at that particular moment as I listened and attempted to recollect my education while paralyzed by mental fatigue, fear, and deep emotional pain: "Wah wah wah Wah wah Wah wah wah Wah wah." My mind could not find comfort in the words of the Catechism, the biblical commentaries, or the classes at seminary. Actually, it all seemed quite cold and abstract. I thought, "Who really cares about fanciful theories and words devoid of feeling when I'm in the midst of intense suffering?" My subconscious replied: "The Word became flesh" (John 1:14).

Theology is simply "faith seeking understanding." If I want to understand my faith, what better way is there than for me to experience it? Perhaps the Word became flesh because we cannot learn what we need to learn through words, but only through life. Maybe the Way was agonizing, the Truth was painful, and the Life was sometimes excruciating. The lessons of the Word made flesh advanced from the happy days of Christmas to the challenges of Good Friday. Now that I can feel, relate to, and learn from.

I'm exactly where I need to be at this advanced stage of faith — crying out with arms open wide willing to experience and receive the pain with no questions asked. That's the experience and the ultimate test of faith that I must be willing to take. There are reminder notes visible to me on every crucifix. If you think about it, it's like an open book test. The answers have been given — the Word has been made flesh.

"In the beginning was the Word, and the Word was with God, and the Word was God. He was in the beginning with God. All things came into being through him, and without him not one thing came into being. What has come into being in him was life, and the life was the light of all people."

John 1:1-4

"Hope deferred makes the heart sick,
but a desire fulfilled is a tree of life."

Proverbs 13:12

The Tree of Life

It happens frequently and usually in the midst of the happiest of days. The sun is shining, and I feel the warmth of its glow on my shoulders. A gentle breeze blows playfully through my hair. In the distance, I hear the cheerful melody of a chorus of birds singing completely out of synch, but quite intentionally. All is calm; all is bright. Then I suddenly hear the giggles of little girls nearby, and without warning, an earthquake shakes the foundations of my soul. Memories rush in and flood my mind like a tsunami wave that engulfs my brain with an uncontrollable force, and the water gushes outward from my eyes and cascades to the ground, taking my joy with it.

For a moment or two or three, I let the tsunami consume me with its reminders of days gone by. With great remorse, I am carried through the murky waters of yesterday as it picks up speed and swallows up everything in its path, leaving no trace of the peaceful place I sat only seconds before. When I have experienced enough pain, I begin to struggle against the force of the waves pull, and I gasp for air and a glimpse of the bright sunlight and blue sky that I know is still there, begging me to return to its warmth. It is not easy to rise above the pull of the surge of memories, however.

In time, the wave recedes, not without causing some damage. Usually my mood has been drastically altered, a seemingly sudden shift to those who are sitting right beside me yet have miraculously escaped the wrath of the tsunami.

I'm too exhausted from fighting against the current to bother to explain the trauma I have just experienced. It takes time, some days more than others, to pick up the pieces of the devastation and return to the safe zone, which is somehow in the exact location where the wave just crashed. I suppose the length of time depends on the size of the wave. Some are more powerful and more consuming than others.

I remember watching the video footage of the Sri Lanka tsunami some years ago. It seemed that often the most immediate help and hope for survival were firmly planted trees. Terrified and powerless people latched onto the large trees and their deep roots for safety and security amidst the forceful flow of the waters, raging and dislocating everything in sight.

Those images are good reminders for me to hold onto the tree of life, which is planted right here and now in the present moment. Its roots run deep and are securely grounded, providing the stability and strength I need to keep me safe. It offers the opportunity to "eat and live forever" (Genesis 3:22). The tree of life is here and now. I must remember to clasp onto it and remain in the peace of the current moment, rather than being swept away by the destructive currents of a tsunami that exists only in my mind.

*"They are like trees
planted by streams of water,
which yield their fruit in its season,
and their leaves do not wither.
In all that they do, they prosper."*

Psalm 1:3

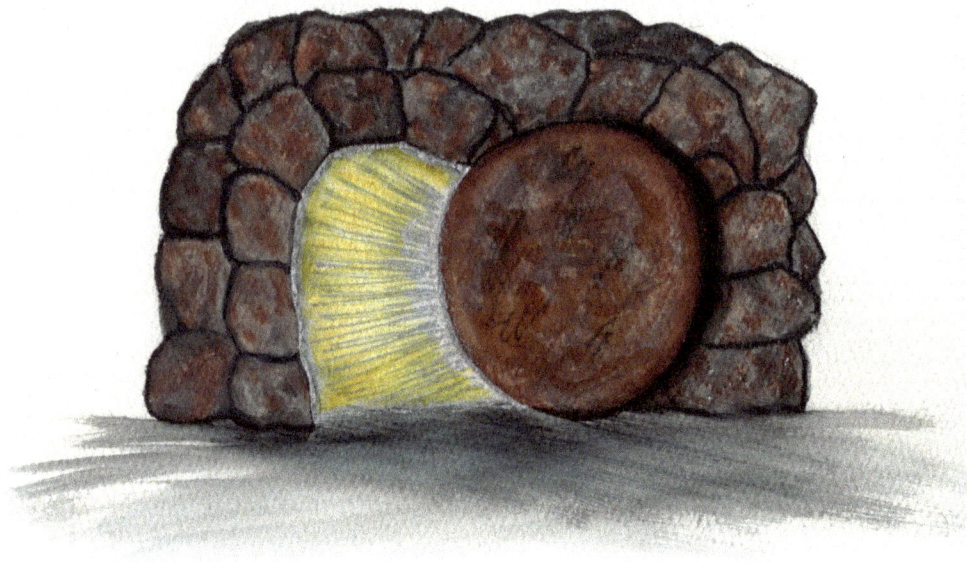

"They found the stone rolled away from the tomb."

Luke 24:2

LEAVE NO STONE UNTURNED

On Easter Sunday, Christians around the world wake with a renewed sense of hope. They do so because over two thousand years ago, a stone was rolled away from a dark, empty tomb, and from the emptiness, new possibilities emerged. Agonizing pain, misery, and the darkness of human nature were replaced by wonder, awe, and excitement. New life, another chance, and a revived sense of meaning and purpose sprang forth from a nothingness that meant everything.

Yet, not all are feeling hopeful this morning. Some may still feel encased, unable to breathe or catch a glimpse of an end in sight. How many are paralyzed beneath the pressure of their circumstances? I wonder how many awoke buried in work, debt, fear, or sadness? There are surely those who are suffering, those who are grieving, and those who are toiling to keep their heads above the weight of their burdens. Life's events can sometimes feel like stones that knock us down, and we can become exhausted from trying to roll them away on our own.

Life's burdens are not meant to be carried or pushed alone, however. We need others to get us through the struggles, accompanying us in our trials and helping us roll away those heavy stones, lest we become exhausted or buried. Even in the gospel story, we hear the concern of the weight of the stone and the inability to move it without assistance. Although there were several people there at the tomb, they still needed more help. Mark 16:3 reads "They had been saying to one another, 'Who will roll away the stone for us from the entrance to the tomb?'"

It's always good to remember that Christianity all started with a community of people who encountered a tragic event and accompanied one another through it. Together they went to pay homage, but they knew there was a stone – a seemingly insurmountable obstacle – that looked like it would stand in their way. They approached the scene together, sad and afraid, but ready to enlist others to help remove the obstacle.

Those who were at the scene of the tomb were blessed. When they arrived, the stone had already been removed for them! There was no need to struggle or fear. They were the first to be set free by the One who showed them the way. The way revealed was self-emptying love, the kind of love that rolls away the stones that entomb faith. They were "amazed" and sent off to share the news so that others too might know and experience the relief, joy, and hope. All was shared with the community so that all could be set free.

Today let's remember to help others roll away those stones that life has cast at them, stones that weigh them down, bury their hope, and kill their faith. Let's leave no stone unturned.

"Bear one another's burdens, and in this way you will fulfill the law of Christ."

Galatians 6:2

"The hearing ear and the seeing eye—
the Lord has made them both."

Proverbs 20:12

Love Sees

Love sees beneath the smile
through the anger
beyond the smugness
amidst the chaos
Love sees.

When fear prefers to look away
or turn around
or follow behind
or point above
Love sees.

When pride chooses to hold her breath
or stamp his feet
or close her eyes
to that which
Love sees.

Love sees the subtle changes
in clothes
posture
hair
voice

The desperate attempts to avoid
attack
blame
deny
Hoping that love will see.

Love sees
and loves
and believes
that love will heal fully
that which
Love sees.

"And a sword will pierce your own soul too."
Luke 2:35

A Mother's Day Fairy Tale

If you do a quick Google search for "Mother's Day," you'll see lots of images of hearts, flowers, and some cute pictures drawn by children signed with the words, "I love you, Mommy." From the images (and Hallmark commercials), it seems motherhood is one big pink bouquet wrapped neatly with a beautiful bow. Today I see those images and feel like I'm being transported to another universe — the same one where geese lay golden eggs and Sleeping Beauty is awakened by the kiss of a handsome prince.

I remember those fairy tale days of flowers, handmade cards, and mornings when two giggling little girls who couldn't wait to bring me breakfast in bed awakened me. Once upon a time, we were a happy, little family living in a modest home in the woods. We took long, peaceful walks and picked wild blueberries in the summer and colorful leaves of various shapes in the fall. We read countless books together on a blanket under the trees, complete with lemonade, of course. We carved pumpkins, made handmade wrapping paper, and decorated the evergreens in our yard with homemade edible Christmas ornaments for the deer, birds, and squirrels. We enjoyed bike rides, hayrides, plane rides, and even exotic cruises. Our days were laden with laughter, playfulness, and deep love.

I've learned, however, that fairy tales and motherhood are not defined by only those simple, joyful moments. We tend to remember the happy endings and forget the pain that occurs in the middle of the story, like the fact that a spell was cast upon

Sleeping Beauty at her sixteenth birthday party, which basically sent her into a coma for one hundred years! The fairy tales, like real life, usually contain frightening circumstances and dangerous predators that intermingle with and threaten the happy ending. There are problems and conflicts, evil beings and disastrous encounters. The ending of the fairy tale is often dependent upon the heroic acts or disposition of the characters. Their response is what makes the story so captivating and timelessly inspiring. Imagine how the fairy tale might have changed if Sleeping Beauty awoke with an attitude of resentment, distrust, and misery!

In life and in fairy tales, it's important to read, experience, and remember the whole story. We gasp when the evil fairy casts the spell on Princess Aurora (Sleeping Beauty), threatening to kill her on her sixteenth birthday. We hold our breath as she grows, hoping the good fairies will be able to keep her safe from harm. We smile as Aurora enjoys her childhood and flits amidst the critters in the forest. We cringe when the evil fairy searches for her throughout the years, threatening the sweetness of her simple life. We weep and mourn when Aurora falls into her deep slumber awaiting fate's sweet kiss of life. We probably forget that her handsome savior was captured by soldiers and attacked by the evil fairy on his way to find Aurora, because all that seems to matter is that he eventually finds and kisses her, and they live happily ever after.

Wherever you are in your story of motherhood, remember it's not over yet. Like all good fairy tales, every mom's story is likely not going to end without times of beauty and joy as well as moments of evil and sorrow. To focus on one extreme and not the other is to potentially miss much. If we stopped reading Sleeping Beauty midway, we might think it was a horror story instead of a fairy tale! All of it — the good and the bad — is part of the story.

We're all living a fairy tale, regardless of the scene we're in at the moment. Thankfully we are unlikely to have to remain asleep for one hundred years before the happily ever after!

"Let them praise his name with dancing,
making melody to him
with tambourine and lyre."

Psalm 149:3

The Dance

For some odd reason, when I was in seventh grade, we had ballroom dance lessons in the gymnasium of my Catholic school. I'm not sure if they were weekly or less frequently, but I remember gathering as a class to learn the steps to dance the Waltz (box step). The teacher called out the steps as we practiced them: "Forward – side – together; backwards – side - together. One two three, four five six; one two three, four five six."

We first learned and practiced individually in straight lines, with the teacher demonstrating the moves in the front row. Once we seemed fairly comfortable with the steps, the teacher played music, and we practiced again, this time in rhythm with the sound of the music. I always liked dancing. I could pick up the steps fairly effortlessly, and I had a pretty good sense of rhythm. So these practice sessions were enjoyable for me!

Then, about once a month, the gym where we learned and practiced was transformed into a ballroom. The girls were lined up on one side of the gym in their dresses and the boys on the other side with their suits and ties. The boys were then told to pick a girl and ask her to dance. I have no idea why this was part of the curriculum, but there you have it! I'm *that* old!

When a boy finally did ask me to dance (it always seemed like an eternity!), I was usually quite frustrated with the dance experience. It was my turn to follow now, but it was very uncomfortable for me to let the boys lead. After all, I was a better dancer, and they usually got the steps all wrong! Needless to say, it didn't feel like a dance at all – more like a chore, a frustrating challenge that kept me unaware of the beautiful background music and left me feeling annoyed and exhausted.

I realized today that I tend to live the dance of my life in much the same way. I'm constantly trying to lead, and I feel that same frustration that I felt in the seventh grade. I think to myself, "This isn't the way the day should go . . . or the project . . . or the relationship . . . or the holiday." I'm constantly fighting against my dance partner, even though I know in my heart that I can trust Him to guide me.

Today I must remember to listen to the music (even when I don't like the melody), to dance with purpose, and not worry if the steps seem out of synch. I must remember to carry on and dance with a joyful heart, so that when the dance is over, I can exhale and rest in the comfort of knowing that I danced my part. I danced gracefully despite the apparent missteps. I listened to the wonderful music, and I fully experienced the exciting swirls and even the surprising and abrupt dips. Throughout the dance of life, I felt the gentle clasp of my partner's hands. I gazed into His eyes with trust, and I simply let God lead.

"You have turned my mourning into dancing;
you have taken off my sackcloth
and clothed me with joy,
o that my soul may praise you
and not be silent.
O Lord my God, I will give
thanks to you forever."

Psalm 30:11-12

"Do not be afraid; for see—
I am bringing you good news of great joy
for all the people."

Luke 2:10

Good News

I've never been one to watch, read, or listen to the news. Still, I always know what's going on in the world through the people in my life. It's usually Mom who calls and says something like, "Did you hear that Oprah is running for president?" "No, Mom," I reply, "I don't watch the news." I wish I counted the number of times she retorted, "The world could be coming to an end, and you would have no idea!" It's really not a matter of disinterest; I just find the news to be rather disturbing. I can't imagine why I'd want to allow such chaos into my home, my safe haven.

Sometimes when I'm at the gym or a restaurant, I'm subjected to the news reports because I can't control what channels are playing there. Every small or large catastrophic, shameful, hateful, or hurtful event in any corner of the world is replayed continually, to the point that it creates an intense level of anxiety and despair that I never would have experienced had I not tuned in! Plus, I have to listen to the opinions of any people the reporters decide to question, who are only more than happy to add their voices to the barrage of those already being embedded in my now very confused brain.

I attended a symposium once where the topic was "fake news." There were several very interesting presentations on the subject, and discussion followed. There were also some pretty heated debates about the credibility and responsibility of news reporters. By the conclusion, I decided that it is really the people who accept and absorb the news that carry the real weight of responsibility. Who was to blame in the narrative of the Garden of Eden? Was it the snake's fault for twisting the message or Eve's fault for accepting the lies and eating the apple?

There has always been fake news, but there's also much authentic and good news. We are never going to eliminate the liars. We can point fingers and try to shift the blame all we want, but in the end, we bear the responsibility for what we accept and do with the deceit and betrayal. Do we stand up for truth when we recognize lies, or do we remain silent and allow the deception to continue? Do we become bitter and resentful when we realize that we have been betrayed, or do we "turn the other cheek" (Matthew 5:39) and learn from the lesson? Do we manifest truth and good news in a way more captivating than those who spread hatred and fake news? Do we obsessively tune in and allow ourselves to be confused and swayed by the reports of others, or do we retreat to a quiet place to discern and carry the truth forward in a way that will change the world?

I'm no worse for the wear having not watched the news all these years. I somehow manage to stay abreast of what's important and make positive changes when I hear news of injustice. When the "snakes" want me to believe that all hope is lost and the world is coming to an end, I choose instead to pause, pray, and reflect on the Good News. The snakes cannot change what I know deep within. It would be much easier for me to blame others, but in the end, I am the one who makes the decision to accept or refuse their lies and to make manifest the light of truth.

> *"How sweet are your words to my taste,*
> *sweeter than honey to my mouth!"*
>
> Psalm 119:103

Taste and See

Pentecost is a day when Christians celebrate the descent of the Holy Spirit on the first members of the Church. We read in Acts 2:3 that the Spirit appeared "as *tongues* of fire." It just so happens that I awoke one Pentecost morning with a sore on my tongue, and it made me wonder, "What is God trying to tell me here?!" So I started thinking further about the tongue — an important muscular organ that I take for granted, especially as a public speaker.

The tongue is vital for chewing and swallowing the food that nourishes and sustains us. Sure, we could still manage to survive without the tongue, but think of all the enjoyable tastes that we would be missing. Today alone I experienced and enjoyed so many flavors, from my morning cup of coffee and chocolate donut at breakfast to the raspberry smoothie I had for lunch. These wonderful flavors are an important part of the otherwise rather dull requirement that feeding my body might be. The flavors transform this necessary sustenance from an obligation into a rewarding experience.

When I was young and newly married, one of our neighbors developed mouth cancer. He had surgery which resulted in the loss of all sense of taste, but fortunately, he could still eat. I was unaware that he had lost his sense of taste, so I baked him his favorite chocolate chip cookies and cheerfully delivered them to him and his wife. His response was not what I expected. He nearly cried when I presented the cookies to him, because he could smell them, but he could no longer enjoy the sumptuous flavors like he once did. I think God intervened that day. My dog ended up eating all the cookies when I left them on the coffee table to console my neighbor!

While we can still survive and nourish our bodies without the tongue, we would certainly not be able to talk. I sometimes experience the frustration of being unable to speak when I have a sore throat. Maintaining healthy relationships becomes much more challenging, because communication is a vital part of cultivating a relationship. I can only imagine how difficult it must be for the people who must endure this suffering permanently. Verbal communication is another gift that we take for granted, and it is dependent on the tongue. That's why when we are having trouble expressing ourselves, we are said to be "tongue-tied."

I can see now the great wisdom of the Holy Spirit choosing to appear as "tongues of fire." What better symbol than the tongue to depict how the Spirit feeds and nourishes our spirits? As "tongues of fire," the Spirit also cultivates our relationship with God and others by communicating that His great love is with us always. The Holy Spirit's tongues of fire remind us that life can be more than simply survival. We can live it abundantly and savor its bountiful flavors (from the sweet to the savory to the sour). Even the most mundane obligations can become rewarding experiences, when we are willing to "taste and see" (Psalm 34:8).

"The good person out of the good treasure
of the heart produces good,
and the evil person out of evil treasure
produces evil;
for it is out of the abundance of the heart
that the mouth speaks."

Luke 6:45

No Words

I once had the privilege of walking down an ancient street in a small medieval town in Portugal. It was a sunny day and extremely hot, a typical climate for the south of Portugal at that time of the year. Cats meandered through the streets along with me, my husband, and groups of other tourists, while the local residents sat in the town center sipping red wine and cold beer. I could hear the sounds of pots clanging as women cooked Sunday meals in their flats, dogs barking in the distance, and the birds sang so sweetly overhead. This is the life, I thought.

Then suddenly I turned a corner, and I noticed one bird that wasn't singing very joyfully. Not only was he not singing, he also wasn't moving. My husband glanced down and continued to walk by as the pigeon lay there frozen. I stopped and began to speak to the bird, forgetting that this was a Portuguese pigeon that clearly could not understand English. Yet I was certain he could understand my good intentions by the gentle sound of my voice as I leaned down to give it some water. It was obvious that the pigeon was injured as he wobbled and stumbled with each little step, but he was very hot and thirsty, so he did his best to move towards the water and drink some. I continued to gently run the water from my bottle, and I splattered some on his feathers to cool him off. He really liked it and seemed to be coming back to life!

My husband reminded me that we had to move on to get our lunch before the tour group left town without us. So we continued walking down the street and up the hill to find a restaurant. We waited quite some time for lunch, and as we sat at the table, I couldn't help but think of the pigeon alone in the street. So I left my husband at the restaurant and headed back to the pigeon with some more water and bread. I made little feeding dishes of water out of the tops of several bottles, and I sat next to the bird on the cobblestone ground. I felt certain I could save him!

Out of nowhere, an elderly local man turned the corner and came towards me and my pigeon friend. He started speaking to me in Portuguese, and I awkwardly tried to explain in English that the pigeon was injured and must be saved. The man and I exchanged words, each in our own language, and I believe we were communicating somehow, although neither of us could comprehend a word the other was saying. He was trying to tell me that the pigeon was sick and was going to die, an outcome that I just could not accept.

So I began making dramatic hand gestures to try to tell him to do something to save the pigeon, and I tried to explain with my index finger that I was sad as I drew an imaginary tear from my eye. The old man wanted to help, so he leaned down and, to my great surprise, turned into an apparent pigeon expert. It was a miracle, I thought, as the man swooped the pigeon up gently in his hands and examined its wings while trying to explain to me (in so many words that I could not understand) that the wings were injured. "No, his foot is hurt," I retorted as I motioned with my hands again pointing to the pigeon's foot. "No," my Portuguese friend replied (that I did understand), "it's the wings."

Before I could stop him, he threw the pigeon up in the air to prove to me it was his wings. Of course, the poor pigeon fell fast to the hot cobblestone ground. I gasped in horror, and the old man shrugged and motioned as if to imply that his assessment was correct — it was the wings. I still couldn't accept it, and I was trying to ask if he could just bring it to an SPCA or something (clearly there was no such service in this small ancient town), so the old man tried again. He scooped the pigeon up, stretched out and examined each wing one at a time, then checked each foot ("yes! yes!" I shouted — "it's the feet!"). "No," the man replied, and again he tossed the bird up to prove it was the wings. This time, the bird not only fell on the hot cobblestone ground; he fell behind a basement window grate! "No!" I gasped. "Take him out of there!" I shouted and motioned.

Still wanting to help both the pigeon and me, the old man reached behind the grate and pulled the pigeon out. I breathed a sigh of relief and began to explain (in English and with lots of hand motions!) that the bird clearly needed water. So the elderly man motioned for my water bottle, took a swig, and began to offer the water from his mouth to the bird's beak. The pigeon and I were terribly disturbed and confused! The man seemed to be a pigeon expert, though, so I watched and felt slightly hopeful about this mouth-to-beak resuscitation of sorts.

Now the man placed the bird gently behind the grate, explaining to me that the bird must die and that spot was the safest for him to do so. I filled the tiny water bottle caps with more water, splattered more on his body, and left lots of breadcrumbs for my little friend. The old man and I turned the corner and climbed the cobblestone hill in silence. Once we reached the top, we went our separate ways, feeling better because we both worked together and did the best we could despite the language barrier. I think the pigeon understood that too.

Though we probably didn't save the bird, I learned a valuable lesson. Communication can be ambiguous and harmful when speaking the same language, and it can be clear and beneficial even when the words that are being spoken are foreign. Perhaps we put too much emphasis on speech and too little on genuine expressions that transcend words. Kindness, gentleness, and concern are expressed in so many ways that are unmistakable by all beings, human and otherwise. It was frustrating at first, not being able to say what I needed to with words, but in the end, the experience was very special because we spoke with our hearts — the man, the bird, and me.

And the Lord said, "Look, they are one people, and they have all one language; and this is only the beginning of what they will do; nothing that they propose to do will now be impossible for them. Come, let us go down, and confuse their language there, so that they will not understand one another's speech."

Genesis 11:6-8

(Maybe God jumbled their speech so they'd have to learn to speak more with their hearts!)

*"Where there is hatred, let me sow love.
Where there is injury, pardon.
Where there is doubt, faith."*

Saint Francis of Assisi

Saints and Stones

I had been wandering around the beautiful town of Assisi, Italy for several days. It's an ancient Umbrian village filled with historic and religious sites, especially those that commemorate the places where Saint Francis once lived, worked, and prayed. Tourists arrive in droves daily to catch a glimpse of the original San Damiano crucifix, pray in the spots where Saints Francis and Claire once prayed, or stand near the tombs of these two great saints. Everywhere you turn, you can read stories about how Francis and Claire lived their lives with a zealous love for God — a love that was so great it still inspires people nearly eight hundred years later.

As I watched the people come and go through the churches and past the tombs, the statues, and the many historic locations, I could sense that they desperately wanted a fragment of the holiness these saints possessed. They wanted to take home the holy water, small San Damiano crucifixes, prayers cards, and anything else that might exude even a small fraction of the grace that Francis and Claire possessed. I sensed the longing in the air. I could feel the desperation. I could see the fervent petitioning as people touched the statues and walls and dropped to their knees in adoration.

I realized as I watched the passersby that we all want the easy way out. We want a guideline for holiness and a clear-cut way to God. We want Francis and Claire to touch us with their spirits here in this place, to transform us in some way by sharing even just a molecule of the grace they received from God. We think holiness is there for the taking if we could just reach out and touch it or if we get close enough to the spirit of those who attained it. We are looking outward for a sign, recipe, or relic, but so few are looking inward. If only all I had to do was to come to a place such as this and inhale the sweet aroma of grace to be transformed by the faith journeys of those who have gone before me.

As I looked more closely at my fellow pilgrims, I realized that in my midst are living stones, and we are here trying to draw spirit from lifeless rocks. I can almost hear Saints Francis and Claire shouting: "Look within! Look to your left! Look to your right! You are the living stones!" (1 Peter 2:5). God is already among you (Luke 17:21), and He was long before you got to this beautiful place. Don't look away from the eyes of your neighbors to gaze into the statues before you. Be inspired by our lives, and then love one another (John 13:34).

Not to worry, we're in good company. Saint Francis began diligently rebuilding a dilapidated physical church when he heard God's voice beckoning him to "Rebuild my church." It wasn't until many years later that he realized God was actually calling him to build up the community that is the Church. Certainly, rebuilding the stone structure would have been simpler than transforming the hearts of the community. However, pilgrims would not come to Assisi if all St. Francis did was repair a building. They come, pray, and marvel because a simple man transformed an entire town and so many around the world throughout the ages with a simple message of love, peace, and all good. It's a message that soars above the buildings, stones, and statues. It is carried far beyond the holy town, as on the wings of eagles by the same Spirit that abides with and in you and me (John 14:17).

*"Like living stones,
let yourselves be built
into a spiritual house,
to be a holy priesthood,
to offer spiritual sacrifices
acceptable to God
through Jesus Christ."*

1 Peter 2:5

"You shall love the Lord your God
with all your heart,
and with all your soul, and with all your mind,
and with all your strength.'
The second is this,
'You shall love your neighbor as yourself.'
There is no other commandment
greater than these."

Mark 12:30-31

Do You Like Me?

I wonder what social media might have looked like in the times of Jesus. I mean Jesus had enough problems with people and friends, and that was when word traveled slowly! Imagine if Facebook existed during those days:

> Post from Jesus: "Healed a leper today."
>
> Facebook friends: 2 likes
>
> Post from Jesus: "Rose Lazarus from the dead."
>
> Facebook friends: 100 new friend requests, 50 likes, and 30 comments of approval. Also, 25 laughing emojis, 2 sad emojis, and 25 obscene comments from haters.
>
> Post from Jesus: "Turned over some tables at the temple courtyard."
>
> Facebook friends: No likes, 20 unfriended, 50 unfollowed, and several obscene comments from haters.
>
> Post from Jesus: "I am going to be crucified. Please pray for me."
>
> Facebook friends: 75 blocked, 25 shameful and hurtful comments, 2 sad emojis.

The thought of Jesus using Facebook in his earthly ministry seems ludicrous, yet how many of us claim that it's all part of the New Evangelization? Is it really possible to touch human hearts and minds through a soul-less medium, or must we work harder to find creative ways to encounter and inspire one another in the flesh?

When we post, like, and friend, we're seeking connection, acceptance, and love, and we somehow believe that is possible behind the screen of a computer or phone. We want friendship to be neat and simple, as easy as the click of a button. The truth of the matter is, however, that friendship is messy. It's going to hurt, maybe even to the point of suffering. Yet, through the painful times, we learn and grow, and we are being molded into (hopefully) better people. These are not lessons we can learn on our own behind a screen — we need to encounter one another.

Real relationships give us an authentic platform to communicate and learn from one another's words, actions, and expressions. It is in the context of real relationships that we say things like: "I will not deny you" (Matthew 26:35), only to discover we are not as strong as we thought we were and learn to ask forgiveness. In real relationships, we can be gently touched in healing and life-giving ways (Luke 7:14-15). We can physically hear (John 11:5-6) and see (John 6:1-15) where help is needed.

Our senses are there to aid us in all that we do, yet the majority of them are being shut down when we sit in the virtual reality of our so-called "friends" on social media. It's time we come to our senses and put those bodily senses back to work, so that we can "taste and see" (Psalm 34:8) all that is truly good, instead of being blinded by the senselessness of virtual "likes."

Let's imagine Jesus on Facebook again. This time he's inquiring about the lack of "likes":

"Simon son of John, do you like me? . . . Feed my lambs."

"Simon son of John, do you like me? . . . Tend my sheep."

"Simon son of John, do you like me? . . . Feed my sheep (John 21:15-18)."

I think Jesus would tell us not to bother "liking" his page, but rather to live like him. Next time I'm on Facebook tempted to "like" a post or count my "likes," I'm going to stop and hear Jesus asking me to get out there and go about the real work of loving, not liking. It's a lot more difficult but much more fruitful. It's what I'm called to do (Mark 12:30-31).

"For we walk by faith, not by sight."

2 Corinthians 5:7

Walk This Way

I generally try to do whatever I can to reduce my carbon footprint. I strive to walk more gently on the earth, always keeping in mind those who have fewer resources available to them. Believe me, I have a long way to go, but I'm really trying to be aware of the way that I live and walk on this planet. I have reduced my energy consumption by keeping our apartment cooler than usual in the winter and warmer in the summer. I collect all of our food scraps in a bucket and deliver them weekly to a compost collection site. I'm certain to turn lights off when they are not being used, and I recycle anything and everything that is recyclable. Like I said, I have a long way to go, but I'm trying.

Lately, I've been thinking about my spiritual footprint. What would a visual map of my footprints look like at the end of my life? Where were the majority of my steps moving? Were there destinations that I frequented often? Why did I frequent them? Was there an intentional purpose? Would there be more steps going to and from the popcorn store downtown than to a sacred place of worship? Would my steps to the coffee shops exceed those that walked toward loved ones and God? How fast or slow was the pace of my steps? How gentle or harsh? Did I rush frantically and mindlessly or slowly and mindfully? Were the times of movement counterbalanced with times of stillness, when I could simply bask in the beauty around me? How often were my footprints replaced by the indentations of my knees falling to the earth in praise and thanksgiving? What would this map of my footprints reveal about me and my unique purpose on Earth?

Truthfully, it makes me a bit uncomfortable to imagine this spiritual footprint map. Too often I'm not conscious of my movement. I am afraid that the steps to the coffee shops, restaurants, and popcorn store might outnumber those to more meaningful places, not to mention people in my life. I wonder how many footprints might be missing because of all the hours I sat behind a computer or gazing at a phone or television. How many times were my footprints frozen in fear?

Starting today, I think I'll keep a record of my footsteps by asking myself a few questions at the end of each day. Where did I walk today? What was the pace of my movement? Did I walk mindfully and gently, balancing my movement with stillness, rest, and prayer? What adjustments do I need to make tomorrow to ensure that my footsteps are heading in the right direction?

Life is a journey. Every step that we take is a gift and an opportunity to move toward or away from our ultimate destination or goal. At the end of my life, I hope to stand before God and hear God say, "Well done. Come celebrate with me!" (Matthew 23:25). I want to have walked by faith (2 Corinthians 5:7) in the way of love (Ephesians 5:2) and as a child of the light (Ephesians 5:8). I must begin now so that the map of my footprints will reveal that my steps moved purposefully and joyfully toward that goal.

"Our steps are made firm by the Lord, when he delights in our way."

Psalm 37:23

www.ninamariecorona.com

www.ingramcontent.com/pod-product-compliance
Lightning Source LLC
Chambersburg PA
CBHW062025290426
44108CB00025B/2787